Did I Hear
The
Voice
Of God?

By Stephanie Devlin

In any country, in any town, live street
sleepers, drug abusers and alcoholics.
This is a true story of two people who
became the hands of Jesus – serving the
ones He loves.

Did I Hear
The
Voice
Of God?

Steph and Geoff Devlin: Curriculum Vitae

We believe that this is a God given book. We have been inspired by the demand of the public in asking for this to be published. We are not envisioning merely a few copies, as we have a world-wide mailing list. Christians and non Christians have requested a copy of the book once in print. When we talk at many hundreds of meetings there is a lot of interest in knowing more about how God has worked in our lives. Similarly, audiences are spellbound by the stories we tell of God's hand on the lives of those we work alongside. We have been honoured for our work by Queen Elizabeth II, national television and numerous radio stations both local and national. We have been awarded on several occasions in recognition of our work. We are Christians. Our work follows the course set by God. Therefore, the appeal of Leamington Christian Mission is inter-denominational – a very wide ecumenical range. Our thirty volunteers come from many different Christian fellowships.

We reach beyond our Christian brothers and sisters, out into the secular world. When they hear of the successes – lives being turned around; former drug abusers and alcoholics learning to live clean lives – organisations and individuals recognise the input of our work and therefore of God. We knew that God had touched lives when a mother came up to us with tears flowing and said: "Thank you! Thank you! If it wasn't for you my son would be dead! He was living a wasted life. And now, look at him – he has just collected his university degree."

Stephanie Devlin

Foreword

Steph and Geoff Devlin are two ordinary people leading extraordinary lives, dealing with the unloved, homeless and hungry. Their world was turned over and shaken sixteen years ago by a vision asking them to step out into the streets of the respectable town of Royal Leamington Spa. They were to feed, clothe and nurture the needy in the name of God – their only resource: faith.

It is a book that tells of the lives of the homeless, the alcoholics and drug abusers; the families who need support; the lonely; the hungry. It speaks of how God gave Steph a vision and how He gifted husband and wife with the faith to put His love into action. The book tells of the impact of God's love through life-changing encounters with the needy. It highlights humour, even in dire situations and triumph in the most desperate of circumstances.

This is a faith mission, supported by a wide network of churches, Christian organisations and individuals, both nationally and internationally. Their large mailing list ranges from Leamington Spa to Norfolk to Tywyn Gwynedd to Stratford upon Avon to Liverpool to the USA, the Netherlands, Kenya, and Australia and beyond!

I expect most people have talents. The gift is in recognising and developing them in yourself; encouraging their development in others.

Steph and Geoff Devlin have been given the gift of a mission to come alongside those who no one else - it seems – wants to know. And what a treasure trove of gifts that mission contains: gifts of caring, hospitality, kindness, gentleness and giving.

Leamington Christian Mission is compelling. It draws the lost, the hungry, the cold, and the lonely. It drew me to become a volunteer on their buses, to share in those gifts whilst trying, inadequately, to give a little of my time. I went along to give and ended up receiving

– but that is part of my story. What follows is Steph and Geoff's story - the writing of it a gift in itself, recognised and encouraged by Steph. I have always wanted to write, yet never ventured seriously upon the journey of beginning to end, until Steph suggested that I might write the story of her life-changing vision and the consequences of obeying it.

My friend and I have spent many days together over many months – Steph talking, me questioning and probing; she delving and remembering, reliving encounters and experiences, me turning her reminiscences, anecdotes, laughter and hopes into written words. We bring you this remarkable story – a gift from He who gives all.

To His Glory.

Anne Horsley – Ghostwriter

This book is a work of non-fiction based on the recollections of Steph Devlin. Some of the names of the people, places, dates and details of events have been changed to protect the privacy of others. The author has warranted to the publisher that, except in such minor respects not affecting substantial accuracy of the work, the contents of this book are true.

Chapter 1

Did I Hear the Voice of God?

Geoff and Steph – Meeting the Need

"Do not neglect to show hospitality to strangers, for thereby some have entertained angels unawares." (Hebrews ch13 v2)

"God bless you. You're an angel."

The gratitude shines out from behind the eyes of the hungry man. His wrinkled hands reach shakily towards the tray; his grimy fingernails evident as he takes from the teeming tray of sandwiches.

"You're welcome, my love."

And he is; they are, all of them. They are most welcome to the abundant food, litres of tea and beakers of "mission" soup served each evening, Monday to Friday, outside the beautiful Jephson Gardens in Royal Leamington Spa. All that is asked in return is a 'please', and 'thank you'; no alcohol; no drugs and no swearing.

The converted ambulance becomes a hive of activity at 6.30pm. Sandwiches are unpacked, or made; soup is poured into plastic cups; tea is stirred; cakes, fruit and puddings are all set out ready to serve. Mountains of quality produce are taken round all the hungry who have visited the bus, offered by us and our team of volunteers.

The atmosphere is bustling and friendly. Dozens of needy folk stand outside, by the railings, or sit on the bench, chatting to their companions, or sitting quietly; whilst others sit inside the larger bus, often listening to Geoff's choice of Christian songs, whilst enjoying their evening meal. The needs are many and varied: some are friendless – we try to provide a smile and a kind word; some come to meet with their friends; some are homeless, sleeping rough and needing a blanket; some are there to seek advice; someone else may need help to answer a letter, or fill out a form. The needs are as numerous as the people themselves. The response is consistent, firm and loving from servants of God doing what God has asked us to do.

1

After fourteen years of being God's operators on the streets of Royal Leamington Spa, we are familiar figures in the town, associated only with our work with the needy. But it was not always so. All those years ago, we led very different lives. Geoff was a well-established butcher, partnering a business; I was a registered childminder, minding disturbed and special needs children; I led the children's work in their church. We were registered foster parents. We led busy, routine lives – until the vision that was to impact upon us both dramatically, changing and upending any preconceived ideas we may have had for our future. God's timing is not always obvious! He sent me a life-changing dream at a time when our lives were at the lowest ebb – at the culmination of two terrible years.

Geoff's stepfather 'Pop' became terminally ill with cancer. We nursed him through his suffering, tending to his needs, unaware that there was to be another tragedy before Pop died.

A dreadful series of events began on Christmas Day 1988, when an urgent call sent me rushing to my sister's house. "It's Dad, Steph. You've got to come now!" My heart raced and I told myself that everything would be all right. But, despite my desperate denials, when I saw the police car outside my sister's house, I knew that he had gone. He had just returned from taking my niece out when he collapsed and died on the kitchen floor; his death instant, like a light being switched off. Although I recognised that Dad had been given, mercifully, a swift, painless death, this was a heavy burden for all the family to bear; the beginning of many difficult circumstances that were to run over the course of the next two years.

Two deaths left two widows, and very little time to grieve. I was then commissioned with the care of my mum and my mother-in-law; with the patient and compassionate mothering of my own daughter as yet another major setback occurred.

Although our daughter and her fiancé had planned a wedding date, in August 1989, and they had bought, decorated and furnished their new home, the bridegroom-to-be decided to postpone the wedding. The day of the original date of the wedding, the young couple went out for the day. One might suppose this was no remarkable thing for two people who were at the point of committing their lives to each other. But instead of terms of endearment and vows of everlasting faithfulness, the bridegroom-to-be broke the devastating news that he no longer wished to marry his fiancée. The arrangements and preparations had been made; a bright future was being anticipated. The decision to cancel the wedding, and the marriage, caused overwhelming distress to our daughter. She needed the same love and attention as might be given to a helpless baby at that time. I found myself sleeping in the same room as her – precious little comfort for my darling child – but it had to be done. It was one of the hardest times for me; I would have preferred to bear any physical or emotional pain personally rather than witness the anguish borne by our daughter at that time.

After a few months had lapsed, it was necessary for the young couple to settle financially, selling their flat, and all the furniture. It was like sorting belongings after a divorce. Soon afterwards, our daughter bought a car, but, after collecting the new vehicle, she was driving with a friend along a country road when one of the tyres blew, rolling the car over, squashing its roof and threatening the lives of the two young women. Although our daughter was badly bruised and shaken, she lived to witness this miracle; whilst her passenger marvelled at the sensation of being "lifted" from the car, as it turned, and being placed on the bank.

A further danger to life happened in April. Just two months after his sister's car accident, our son was admitted to hospital with a recurrence of the Erythema multiforme syndrome with which he suffered periodically when he was much younger. Although this problem necessitates an additive-free diet, alongside adrenaline and steroid treatment, unfortunately, when admitted to hospital, he had been given instant mashed potato, causing the young man to choke as his throat swelled. Thank God that we arrived to visit him just in time to stop him from choking to death!

As if these life-threatening situations were not enough, I also suffered a traumatic illness. In April of that year I was to be found reeling and collapsing from searing pain, necessitating a pain-killing injection to counter what was thought to be the effects of the endometriosis from which I had suffered for years. Despite the drugs, my condition deteriorated, and when a member of our fellowship, who was a nurse, visited me later, Geoff was advised to call the doctor again. I was rushed into hospital and given an emergency operation on what turned out to be a perforated appendix and a burst ovarian cyst, resulting in the removal of not only the appendix, but also the ovary and the fallopian tube on one side. Geoff was horrified to be told that had he not taken me to hospital at that moment I would have died! Six months later, in October, having been in hospital a further three times, I finally had a hysterectomy.

Although we might have dealt with the deaths of our fathers, being resigned that there is "a time to be born and a time to die", this catalogue of terrible trials caused a grief seemingly too awful to bear. It was one that tested our faith to the limit. It was as if we were under attack – during a sequence of major onslaughts. I wondered how much more we could take. I was devastated emotionally, and exhausted. One Bible verse reminded me to hold on, but I had my doubts! *"In all things, God works for the good of those who love Him."* No matter what dreadful things were happening to our loved ones, and us, we had to trust that God was working out His purpose in all this, and that it may all make sense one day. It was then, at that dreadful time, that God spoke vividly, asking me to upend our lives and step out in faith for Him!

Chapter 2

The Vision

"I will pour out my Spirit on all flesh, and your sons and your daughters will prophesy. Your young men shall see visions and your old men shall dream dreams."(Acts 2)

They lay like litter, cluttering the ground – unwanted, discarded, sneered at, dirty, smelly, unloved. And, as I dreamed, I knew that God was putting His finger on me and saying: "I want you to help these people."

I stepped, bemused, through an old hall, a hall that had part of its walls tongue and groove panelled, painted with that dated duller-than-apple green. And I searched my heart. The response to such a command was definite. When you are hanging on to God with your fingernails; when your life has been churned and turned by a series of heart-rending events, the only answer I wanted to give was "NO!"

Over the course of the next six months I battled with God; I put my excuses and reasons to Him, and He moved each one aside with gentle firmness. He opened doors of possibility and prepared the way so that all my arguments were as nothing.

I muse at how God picks His servants. God and I were at a great distance from each other when I was given that dream. How could I, such an inadequate and insignificant person, with all my problems, have the time, talents or treasures to do what I was being asked to do? I decided to follow Gideon's lead – I laid a fleece and told no one of the dream. If this really is you, Lord, then please confirm it. Just like Gideon, I was protesting: "Why pick me? I can't do what you ask!"

Just before midnight on New Year's Eve, followed by the breaking of bread to welcome in the New Year, it was the custom at our Church to invite members to give testimonies. On the last evening of 1990, Peter, the pastor, asked Geoff to give his testimony. Geoff was so downhearted, because of all the troubles encountered over the previous two years he refused. When I was asked, I accepted, warning Peter that I intended to testify to all the problems and heartache we had coped with. I shared everything that had happened, apart from the vision. I said only that I knew God had a work for us, but at that time I was not prepared to divulge it. That night a tape-recording was made of the service – this had never been done before. When my friend, Netta, heard it, she called me to her house. I was puzzled – what had Netta been listening to? As we sat together, sharing a cup of tea by the fire, Netta told me, in detail, what God had in mind! I was amazed, battling with a host of mixed emotions.

I had given God a firm "No!" in response to the vision. Despite the fact that the vision kept recurring and niggling during quiet times, I continued to push it aside: "No, Lord. How can you expect me to look after the homeless and outcast when Dad and Pop have just died? When we feel bereft, and our Mums need looking after? How can I do this when my daughter and son need me? Who will pay the mortgage now that Geoff's business affairs are in such trouble? And Lord, I enjoy a comfortable lifestyle at the moment. That might have to change, and I'm not sure that I want it to! And how will the bills be paid? And I can't possibly do this on my own, and with Geoff at work there's no one to help. And what about my health? No, Lord, I can't possibly cope!"

Yet, through Netta, God had highlighted the need, and His will for us once more. The response: "It's only a dream" was obviously not appropriate any more. The vision could not be dismissed. It must be seen for what it was – a Godly command. This was a life-changing realisation. This was the answer to the test. I had asked God to show me that this really was His will. At the moment Netta revealed that the vision had been shown to her, she became God's messenger. I had said, "How can you send me, Lord? I am only an ordinary person. I can't possibly do what you ask." The reply was clear now: "My child, you can do this if I help you." The fleece had been dampened. I had my answer, and my reassurance. My friend and I hugged one another and cried.

Looking back, I understand that God allowed us to be put under trials and tribulations only to the extent that we could bear. He took us to the edge – the edge of suffering; the edge of faith – with the result that we both bore experiences that we might use later in our work for Him. And He blessed us with a sure knowledge that He is there for us always. At the moment of realisation that it was God offering this work to us, I saw myself as tiny, helpless child held lovingly in the palm of my heavenly Father's hand. I am protected and borne up. There is nothing I need bear on my own. God is the ultimate provider, carer and strength-giver. For, alongside the vision, and all the hard work it promised, God blessed us with the gift of faith.

God has given me a gift of faith for this time, to say that I don't have to worry about money. I was a worrier; I would worry about not having something to worry about. We gave things up so that God could give through us. Into His hands went the mortgage, community charge, gas, water and electricity bills; even the food that we ate. We had to step out in faith. It was a relief. I was given that peace that passes all understanding. I was stepping from my world to God's dimension. I had a new boss. I became as a little child with a Father who would care for me and provide. I didn't have to do anything. I didn't ask for anything. All I had to do was receive. It wasn't until I took that step, made the decision to follow the vision that I had that amazing feeling.

It seemed that there were no arguments left to give. Our lives were given to God once more, and He turned them around like eddying leaves in the autumn breeze. In October 1990 I was recovering from a hysterectomy. In January 1991 I was climbing fences with a flask of soup!

7

Chapter 3

Snow, Damp and Three Alcoholics

God does not always choose His servants because they are the most experienced or the most knowledgeable. It is fortunate for us that God sees potential! In our case, we were as green as grass – knowing nothing of the work that we had been asked to do. In some ways this was a good thing; it meant that we had to rely on God for every door to be opened through which we could step in faith. From the outset, we decided that because this was God's desire, and His work, then nothing about it should be of man. It was God's orchestration and His tune. Therefore He must conduct and lead.

Since God is a God of order, we felt that it was important to approach the authorities in both the Church and in Leamington Spa to seek their approval and inform them of the work. Firstly, Peter, our Pastor at the Charlotte Street Pentecostal Church was asked to give his blessing to the work, which he did willingly. The support he offered was twofold: prayer, and correspondence with all the churches in the locality, informing them of our intentions – it was not possible for the church there to give financially. Although money had once been an important factor in my life, I now knew, that because this was God's mission field, He would do the providing. What a change from the practical, organised mentality that would previously have seen me worrying about where the financial backing was coming from! Once Netta and I had shared our revelations, it was as if I had been stripped of all anxiety concerning material provision. To this day the handing over of all matters – spiritual, personal and practical – has been total. God is generous with his gifts. To vision had been added faith and reassurance that all needs would be met. Therefore, the prayer support was welcomed without reservation as a vital component of the success of this work.

Secondly, mindful that the Bible urges that the law of the land be kept, we went to speak to the community officer stationed at

Leamington Police station at the time. When he asked us why we wanted to work with the homeless, I began to panic! I knew I must give God His due consideration, yet was convinced that this policeman would think us deranged for wanting to step out onto the streets of Leamington in His name. Why was I concerned? For God had prepared the way in that police station – the community officer was a born-again Christian, who was studying to further his lay ministry! Another blessing was given to the work. Permission was given for us to scale the fences of the prestigious Jephson Gardens. Another door had been opened.

It was with both relief and delight that we met with an enthusiastic response, and an offer of help from Philip Mountain, who was the lieutenant with the Salvation Army in the town. We had been aware that any work with the homeless up to that point, had been carried out by that long-established organisation, and had not wished to tread on anyone's toes. Again, there were no problems; Lieutenant Mountain welcomed the venture and volunteered his services one night a week.

And so, all things having been put in order, I waved goodbye to Geoff and our friend Vernal, on the evening of January 17th 1991. Yes, I stayed behind, reluctantly, because Geoff did not want my safety to be risked in uncharted territory. Instead, Geoff and Vernal, armed with large flasks of soup and tea, and a car boot full of blankets trudged the snow-clad streets for hours looking for people in need. By 2.00am the following morning, cold, and questioning my vision and conviction, they were on the verge of going home. Then, having scaled the fence to Jephson Gardens, they came upon an arched shelter that once stood there. And there, lying on a sodden mattress and covered with one blanket, were three sleeping alcoholics: Steve, Gill and George – their first customers! As the two men encountered these blue-cold mortals, Geoff was amazed that human beings could live like this. He had expected them to be at least under some cover. Geoff asked them something he has found himself repeating thousands of times since: "Hello, are you hungry? Would you like some tea, or soup? Would you like a sandwich?"

You may think that being wet, freezing and hungry might have endeared Geoff and Vernal to the three rough sleepers. Yet, far from welcoming the two friends for their kindness and generosity, the three were, at first, hostile and abusive. They made racially offensive remarks to our friend Vernal, whose response was characteristically tolerant, calm and understanding. Steve was never to be rude to him again.

Geoff and Vernal had encountered three of the most hardened alcoholics in the neighbourhood. One of them, it was later discovered, had once been imprisoned for murder. They were so drunk as to be out of touch with reality, and faced with two strange men in the middle of the park in the middle of the night, offering refreshment from a flask, they were not sure whether to trust them or not! The following night I went with them, since Geoff felt it proper that a woman should minister to a woman.

So here at last was the opportunity to minister to those God had told me to seek out. My heart moved in a melting pot of emotions. Apprehension – how would this meeting go? What would the people be like? Would I be able to deal with them? Excitement – this was the fulfillment of a vision; it was really happening! Resignation – God had set His seal on this work; everything would be fine.

And yet my feelings were to be shaken by the reality of Steve, George and Gill. For we were confronted by three blue-cold human beings; snow-bedded mortals with dampness to lie on. Who was I? What difference could I possibly make by giving them food and blankets? These three represented a huge problem, one that I could only scratch the surface of with my flask and sandwich. They would be here for many years to come unless homes, or a hostel could be found. And what of others? There must be others like these. How could we reach them? How could our small effort give their lives a better quality? I brooded on how Steve, George and Gill came to be in this predicament. Surely they had families. Why weren't *they* helping these ones? What circumstances had led these freezing, bedraggled people to live like this? They were human beings – no different from me, and yet I had a comfortable home and a cozy bed, warmed by an electric blanket. As we made our way home that night, my heart was aching with feelings of inadequacy. My prayer was a desperate one: "Lord, what do you want me to do? What can I say? How can I make a difference?"

George was the easiest out of the three original homeless to deal with, but Steve and Gill made our task very difficult. In one sense they did not know what our agenda was. They could not comprehend why such folk would bother to give of their time and resources to find, feed and care for them. And then they would try hard to manipulate us into giving them whatever they required. It was a learning curve for both them and us. They needed to come to terms with the fact that we were there to serve them out of love – unconditionally. We had to learn to handle them – their alcohol-induced moods; their foul language; their attempts to influence the way we worked. I had to deal with an initial fear of Steve especially. Although he never shouted at me (or any other woman) he had an aggressive edge to his voice and his language was choice. Those early days set a precedence for future contacts with hundreds more needy people to come; they equipped us with people skills; they taught us how to come alongside the most trying of human beings, and yet to love them.

There were to be many, many more like Steve, George and Gill, and many more cold, damp nights. From then on, and for more than two years to come, we, together with our volunteers, sought the needy on seven nights a week. In those early days, we began work at 6.00pm and finished no earlier than 11.00pm. We carried soup and tea and blankets in a bag and served the needy wherever they might be found – in shop doorways, in derelict buildings, in woods, in the hollow of a holly bush!

In those early days, the homeless had to be looked for. We would all walk around the parks of Leamington and Warwick, looking on benches and under bushes. There used to be a huge holly bush in the Jephson Gardens, which had its waxy, waterproofed leaves on the outside, and a sizeable hollow inside. It could be entered by a 'doorway' consisting of a break in the foliage facing away from the

11

main pathway walked by visitors. As we sought the needy, we would often approach the holly bush cautiously, unsure whether it was occupied or not. There, in the darkness, a pair of eyes might appear unexpectedly, causing us to jump in surprise! On rainy nights the homeless would be able to shelter for up to six hours before the rain filtered through the spiky vegetation. On dry nights their wet belongings could be hung on the inside branches – nature's wardrobe put to good use!

The early links made with the Leamington branch of the Salvation Army were very valuable in those first days and weeks. Having one of their Lieutenants working as a volunteer gave a useful access to their washing facilities. Saturday mornings were "wash days". Steve, George and Gill could complete their ablutions and have a change of clean, dry clothes.

There seemed no harm in sharing the locations of these favourite sleeping places with concerned people, until it became clear that the authorities were learning about them too, and had begun making it impossible for the homeless to gain access. The holly bush was fenced; derelict buildings were cleared and demolished, or reoccupied; car parks were gated and wardens employed to discourage unwelcome 'visitors'. We learned that not everyone respected the privacy of those we had been called to serve. It was time to keep quiet about where they stayed.

Similarly, when the local newspapers asked us to give an interview about the Mission, I thought that this could be a real opportunity to share the vision, and how this work was being done for God. The printed article made no mention of the Lord's intentions. The reporter had asked members of the council about their feelings regarding the Mission, and it was reported that our actions had brought these 'undesirables' into the town – that they had not been present before this work had begun! The interviewees from the authorities claimed that the homeless and alcoholics had been attracted by our work, not that we had found these people. They said also, that there was not a housing problem in Leamington; that the homeless did not exist – how could they be since they were not on record. Here we were in agreement: indeed, the homeless were not recorded on the council computer, but they were living right outside the council offices on benches and in the holly bush! What the article did not verify was that the homeless in question had either been raised in or around Leamington, or had family in the town. At the time, the article was hurtful. For us this work had the blessing of the highest authority. It was a gift to Leamington Spa. The fact that others did not see the Mission in such terms was hard to bear. And yet through even these negative comments the Mission was given public exposure, and God's purpose worked for the good. As the mounting collection of clothing, blankets and household items grew inside our house, it was becoming obvious that more and more people and organizations had heard of the work of the Mission, and had things they wanted to donate. Although the newspaper article had caused upset, the situation had been turned around; support for the work was growing in the form of these donations. Sometimes we think we know best. It had seemed a good idea to give this interview to the press, and my vanity was shaken when the outcome appeared to be negative. But I did not see through God's eyes – I did not see the full picture. Once again He was working out His purpose for the good of those who loved Him.

The article opened another door. The council contacted us, asking us to be a point of contact for the homeless. After all, they could hardly send a letter to "The homeless, The Holly Bush, Jephson's Gardens"! Through this role, we were taught how to fill in the necessary forms; we learned how the points system worked – a system, which, in those days, calculated the needs of the individual for housing provision. This newly acquired skill was to be very useful in aiding many homeless people in the future. We were asked to take the needy along to the housing department, to petition for them.

Chapter 4

You'll Never House Me, Steph!

Despite disparaging remarks from a local newspaper, God took the criticism and turned it for good, *"For we know that in all things, God works for the good of those who love Him, who have been called according to His purpose." (Romans 8 v28)*

The reaction of the homeless to the possibility of having permanent shelter and accommodation was incredulity. "You'll never house me, Steph," countered Steve.

"We'll see," was my reply.

Steve, one of the first to be found in that cold, stone shelter, was the first to be housed. He loved the home that he had felt certain would never be found for him. He became extremely house proud, keeping his flat immaculately clean and tidy. In the absence of a fitted carpet, he laid pieces of carpet that had been given to him; in the absence of a vacuum cleaner, he swept the carpet with a toilet brush that he set aside especially for this purpose! In his cutlery drawer his knives, forks and spoons were laid out like soldiers. A new broom swept clean in more ways than one: Steve became sober. He had a new home; a new way of life; a new chance – all brought about by love and a belief in a God of new chances. He had also found a sanctuary in which to welcome his newfound friends. He needed to talk, to feel wanted and accepted for the person he was; he did not need to be judged. He had had years of judgmental comments and actions against him and now thrived on being accepted, unconditionally.

Steve lived in his flat for many years. He began to build relationships once more with people he had lost touch with through his years in prison and living on the streets. He had even started to work. Life was starting to pick up. Then, little by little, he began to allow some of his old alcoholic friends into his flat, and with them came Dave. Dave was a bad influence on Steve. Steve's drinking became worse, and with it his aggressive tendencies, including fights with Dave. Our visits to Steve's flat diminished as his association with Dave grew. It was too dangerous for us to go near. Therefore we did not know that Steve had failed to fill in his housing benefits form. This was a document that had to be filled in annually if a person was on income support, so that the claimant might continue to be housed without paying any extra. Once it was realised that Steve had omitted to complete this form, he had accrued several months of rent, which the housing department insisted was paid. They held that Steve's situation could have changed, and that therefore he had rent arrears. Steve was evicted. He returned to living on the streets. During the floods of 1998 he floated out of Jephson Gardens on his bedroll – his unconscious body in an alcoholic stupor.

I have an enduring picture of Geoff kneeling to wash Steve's filthy, smelly and sore feet, drying them with care and dressing them with clean socks and waterproof shoes. This was the level of care required of us. We, the Devlins, from relative affluence; from a warm, clean house; from dancing in glitzy ballrooms – we were now waltzing in God's formation, to His music. No one could have told us that we would have been doing such things! We would have shunned the very suggestion. Yet God had prepared our hearts. He had opened our eyes to see what lay beyond the alcohol and the dirt. He had given us insight and love to share. This was His love – a love in action.

When Gill and George were housed, Gill proved herself to be a wonderful housewife. She loved to be clean herself. Even whilst sleeping rough she had maintained her personal cleanliness despite seemingly impossible conditions. She would even wash her hair in the cold water of the public conveniences rather than be dirty. However, we had much to learn about the scruples of someone who is dependent upon drugs or alcohol! For, having found someone who would give a second-hand fridge freezer to George and Gill, and having taken it to their new home, we were horrified to visit them one day to find it had disappeared. As we questioned Gill and

George, we discovered that they had sold the appliance to raise money to fund their drinking habit! Thereafter we had signs written on furniture and appliances declaring that it was the property of Leamington Christian Mission.

As we made daily visits to their new home, Gill and George would open up and reveal the stories behind their circumstances. Gill had had a home, two children and a common-law husband who used to hit her. As she turned to drugs and alcohol to escape this nightmare situation, she jeopardized her relationship with her daughters, and they were taken, firstly into care, and secondly adopted. The slippery downhill slope to street sleeping was the consequence of a life fuelled by a drug-induced self-loathing. It was at this point in her life that we came into contact with Gill.

*****

"Get me out of here! They're coming at me with an axe! Get me out of here, Steph!" George's screams filled the building as he struggled to deal with the hallucinations brought on by alcohol. His recent, successful attempts to stop drinking had slipped backwards and frightening scenes of imaginary attackers were now wracking his body. As we raced to the hospital, George continued to rant: "They're following us, Steph! They're coming to get me!" I prayed with him as we drove.

"Do you trust me, George?"

"Yes, Steph, I do trust you."

"Then look me in the eyes. I am telling you that there is no one following us. Just remember what's going on inside you at the moment." George continued to struggle with the horrendous pictures and fears that were besetting him. All I could do was sit with him and be his friend. But his lifestyle had taken its toll on his body; he had a massive stroke from which he has never recovered.

Gill found it very hard to be alone when George was hospitalised. Her already low self-esteem hit rock bottom when her partner became so ill. She renewed her habit of self-mutilation. There were many times when we would meet Gill just walking along the road with arms red with her own blood. Then I would bind her arms with cloths and rush her over to casualty. However, there were times when her efforts were frustrated. On one such occasion, we had taken one of our administration team to show her some of the outside work, but when we visited Gill, she had broken a pane of glass from her flat and was trying to slash her wrists. Our volunteer was horrified, and stared incredulously as I appeared not to be preventing her from hurting herself.

"Stop her, Steph! You've got to stop her!" Sometimes, as experience has taught us, there is nothing we can do when someone is threatening to harm themselves. Their action is a symptom of their own self-hatred, and a cry for help, and, until they do something harmful to themselves, we cannot respond other than by talking and praying.

What our volunteer had not realised was that the safety glass was not cutting Gill's arm, neither were the rounded ended scissors that she tried next, nor the safety razor that was the final "weapon" of self destruction. And each time her attempts failed, Gill's anger grew, until she realised the futility of her actions, so that by the time we had calmed her down she no longer wanted to hurt herself.

The poor volunteer was not enamoured with this part of our work. She decided to stay by her typewriter in future!

*****

It was no accident that Geoff and Vernal could find no one but Steve, Gill and George on that first night. No one else would have served God's purpose at that time. For, in encountering these three needy, angry, disturbed people, Geoff and Vernal had been led to the "king pins" of rough sleepers. They were hardened to life by their backgrounds, and by acute alcoholism. Therefore, once they had realised the practical love that was being provided by us and our volunteers, they were best placed to reassure others in the same predicament; trust grew, and with it the need for the Mission became ever more apparent. A steady stream of needy people approached us. Sometimes, as in the case of Enid and Edward, their requests were fuelled by fear that can accompany mental health. When Enid came down to the bus one evening, I could tell that something was troubling her. Her usual fretfulness was aggravated, and I knew that she needed to talk. Her story was disturbing.

Pulling the blanket over her head kept off some of the cold draughts, but it could not stop the dampness, or the musty smell that spoke of nights of use out in the open. Enid dozed once more, glimpsing the children's swing as her eyes batted their way to slumber. This was a familiar pattern, this snatching of rest as her aching body felt the ungiving concrete that had become her bed of late. Edward's rasps filtered through to her half awakeness; she began to drift into an uneasy dream state. She was aware of his stocky body shifting restlessly. She was glad he was there. To be here, in this place, in the dark and chill was bad enough. To be alone did not bear thinking of. In her shaky slumber world she must have dropped a glass, because her fingertips bared themselves to the rawness of a fresh gash. They gave out the dull, deep soreness of a new wound. The chewing continued – strange how she could carry on eating when she had just hurt herself. She was so clumsy. Her husband used to chide her about breaking things. And then he would . . . Fear rose. Confusion took its familiar place in her head. As her fingers slid compassionately along the ridge then the bones of her little finger, she sensed ripples of hair, short and bristly. It encased a round and bony form, which twitched rhythmically as her pain increased. Enid's dream ceased abruptly. In the yellow dimness spread by the street lamp, her eyes made out three feasting rats. Her screams woke Edward; her vigorous and fervent shaking released the rodents.

Enid and Edward needed dry blankets, clean clothes and food. They needed care and support. They needed a shelter. When we found them sleeping in that children's park, we were able to offer all those things, some immediately, some eventually. But the support continued on a regular basis – about three times a week. Like many who have mental health problems, they required provision and protection. They were recipients of a flat, furniture, bedding, clothing, food and presents. They, alongside fifty others in those early days, received food hampers and gifts at Christmas – a practice that we have been able to continue throughout the time of Leamington Christian Mission.

On one of our regular visits to their flat, we found Edward to be very unhappy. He sat, head in hands and then wringing his hands. Enid was pacing back and forth, then in and out of the bedroom. Edward was ill. He was fretful and disturbed. His schizophrenia was becoming unmanageable. Time to take charge. "Right then. Let's have a cup of tea shall we?" I had to calm the situation; to make them feel that everything would be fine. "Don't you worry. We'll send for the doctor." It was important to take control for the sake of these anxious, nervous people who had become a part of our lives.

And so Geoff and I sat and chatted quietly and gently with them until the doctor arrived, and gave us the inevitable verdict that Edward would need to be sectioned under the Mental Health Act, and hospitalised.

A little while later "Love in Action" was being blazoned up the hill to Hatton Central Hospital as we drove the bus and its fragile passengers. The hospital was prepared for its new patient, the nurses went with Enid to settle him onto his ward, knowing that he would be cared for there.

Enid appeared relieved that her partner was being looked after, and so, after a little while of sitting with her until the early hours of the morning, we said 'goodnight' and went home. How naïve we were. Nowadays we would not leave a mentally disturbed person alone at night – especially one who was used to having a constant companion. But in those green days we did not have the experience to predict what would happen to someone in Enid's predicament.

Enid cried for help as she sat on her own later that night. She took an overdose of pills then rang 999. When we went to check on her the next day, we discovered that an ambulance had taken her to

Warwick hospital. Enid needed looking after, so she had taken matters into her own control, and arranged a way to receive it.

Enid and Edward enjoyed the comforts of their sixth floor flat for about two years. Edward decorated it in his own individual fashion, not worrying about the accuracy of lengths of wallpaper, or about the pattern matching. They kept washing in their bath, and endured the lack of outlook afforded by the high windows. Yet they were warm, clothed and well fed – a far cry from the nightmares of the children's play area.

The door that had been opened stayed open as we took one after the other to seek for homes to take them from the cold, damp dirtiness to warmth and a sense of belonging. In those days the council housing system was generous to the likes of Steve, George and Gill, Enid and Edward. It provided homes that gave these people the chance of a new lease of life.

Similarly, it led us to consider the long-term requirements of those newly housed. We thought it prudent to have electricity and gas meters installed so that power could be paid for as it was needed. Although there were no problems installing the electricity meters, at that time it was the policy of the gas board to provide meters only for people who were two quarters in arrears. Of course, this arrangement would have been counter-productive for our people; but when the lady from the gas board, asked: "Who are you?" She was told: "Geoff," She enquired further: "Not Geoff and Steph?"
"Yes, that's right. How do you know?"
"I've heard of you, and of the good work you are doing. Yes, you can have your gas meters fitted." . . . Another obstacle had been overcome! When Steve had his gas meter fitted we were overjoyed to discover that angels can be gas fitters! After the meter had been fitted we noticed that £10 had been credited to his meter. God's hand reaches into ordinary lives and the small things that affect us.

Chapter 5

From Rats and Fleas to a Bright Red Carpet

Those hidden and forgotten began to be revealed as we became known and trusted by the homeless and needy. Through contacts with Steve, Gill and George, we started very close relations with many others in similar positions – sometimes the needing/giving relationships lasting for many years. Many of the ones we met in those early years were severe alcoholics. It was whilst we were searching for one such person, called Gunner that we came upon Ethel. She was an old lady with mental health problems, who had allowed Gunner to "skipper" (sleep) in her house in Leamington. Our first encounter was in the February of the first year of the Mission. It was a memorable one!

Having found the house, Geoff, Vernal and myself were greeted not by a person, but by an unbearable stench from the bin standing on the step. "Bro!" exclaimed the repelled Vernal. "There's dead flesh in here; I think we ought to go!" We thanked God that no one answered the door!

Not to be deterred, we returned another day, feeling reassured to find no bin outside. The relief was short-lived. When the door was opened to us, there, in the hall was the offending receptacle, complete with malodorous contents! Before us was a household in darkness and coldness. It was a place inhabited by Ethel: an unwashed, incontinent woman who suffered from schizophrenia. Her body, her hair, her clothes were filthy, reeking of human effluence. Her cat and its fleas, rats, mice and their combined waste shared the house, alongside Gunner and any homeless folk who had persuaded Ethel to allow them to doss down wherever they could find a space. The stink from this house of horrors tore at the lining of the nose; it made throats sore; it made it necessary for us to learn to breathe without inhaling fully.

21

"Lord, what have you brought us to? Is this really what you want us to do? This wasn't in the vision. Lord give us strength if this is what you want us to do. You know me better than I know myself. Can I really do this? I'm a lady of order. I like to be clean and tidy; I like to wear high-heeled shoes. What have I come to? Where do I start to help this lady? You are going to have to show me. I can't do this on my own."

True to God's word, that's exactly what He did. I began to see myself in the palm of His hand once more – His helpless child, dependant upon His strength. There was no other way to go about this work. This lady is God's child, just as we are His children. She needed the care, that only God could give; and this was our calling: to provide the hands to do it. If we stop and dwell upon these things in our own strength, it's impossible, but God gives us the ability through faith, to accomplish His work, even down to the basics of relearning to breathe. When I saw Ethel through the eyes of God I saw her as He sees her – not a dirty old lady. Her smile lit up her face. How could anyone resist such beauty!

Here I must pause to explain that we have often found ourselves in situations through which we can see humour. Yet we do not laugh at the misfortune of those we meet; rather, we laugh through it. Finding humour in heartache makes it easier to bear. Out of tragedies come lighter moments, in which the main players say or do laughable things. The amusement does not lessen the reality; neither does it diminish our love for that person. In many ways it enables us to accept that person for who they are, and to love them anyway. We laugh with the people we meet in an effort to turn their situations around.

It is hard to imagine that we might discover anything remotely funny in Ethel's house. Yet we were amazed to encounter various characters skippering in Ethel's over inhabited abode, who helped to lighten the load. One such person was Nina; our first meeting with her etched on my memory – an image framed in the doorway. This was a female who could not be ignored! A lady of ample proportions, Nina's head was swathed in a piece of net curtain, her long, lank hair falling beneath it. She swaggered her hips side to side, swaying her well-proportioned breasts, barely concealing them in her malodorous, low-cut dress. As she held aloft a tatty frying pan that was decorated with the kind of flowers found on canal boat hardware, she announced loudly that she was a gypsy. She then regaled us with her gypsy stories. She insisted that she came from a long line of gypsies. She, of course, was there to care for and help the poor unfortunates inside Ethel's house. She herself, we must understand, did not need our help, since she was of royal gypsy descent.

Her penchant for the opposite sex was obvious as she ogled my husband and our male volunteer! The prospect was worrying, but we had a job to do. However, there were times when her lasciviousness was blatant, as our male volunteers can testify.

Over the months following, Nina came to accept help from us, as she realised that she was accepted by us for who she was. The "Gypsy Queen" act had been dropped. She had become part of the core of people who we met with regularly. On one occasion we were checking the properties rented out by the council to our needy friends when we came across "the gang", Nina being amongst them. Her eagerness to request help was immediate: "Geoff, I need a new bed. I'm being bitten. They're eating me alive. LOOK!" At which point she emphasised the urgency of her need by lifting up her jumper and revealing her welt-covered naked torso! "Eyes up, my darling! You need to look up to the ceiling now!" My advice to my embarrassed husband was timely. My lips twitched with suppressed laughter as Geoff tried to walk hastily from the room with his head aloft.

There was endless teasing of our male volunteers about Nina's attraction to the opposite sex – or of how they might go about the diplomatic avoidance of her advances. She once appeared worse the wear for drink, propped up against the low wall outside Jephson Gardens, and trying to locate her mouth with a cup of soup and a sandwich. Her thin summer blouse was low cut and lacking in support. As she struggled to control her listing body as it slid unceremoniously towards the pavement, so too did certain parts of

23

her upper torso show signs of revealing themselves to all. I could see what was about to happen. "You'll have to go and tell her what's happening, Geoff." I could not resist mocking the men on our team. "Under no circumstances am I doing that! You're kidding!" Geoff gave his shuddering response in no uncertain terms. Perhaps something terrible was about to attack him? "Well somebody has to tell her." Geoff's voice rose to hail one of our volunteers: "Mark! Go and help Nina!" But there was a trail of dust where Mark had once stood. Needless to say, I went out to help Nina restore her dignity.

When she had gathered herself sufficiently to walk over to the bus to request more soup, Nina, soup cup in hand, soup dribbling down her front, spied Mark and her eyes turned wide and interested. "Ooooo! Mark!" The words were meant to be sweet and endearing, but Mark was not impressed. His shaking knees were the give-away. When she followed up her greeting with a proposition to take him into the gardens and show him a good time, Mark's fear turned to action – he retreated faster than a jack rabbit being chased by a hound. Netta and I had to remain for a while with our heads shoved in the cupboard until our bodies had ceased quaking with uncontrollable giggles at poor Mark's plight.

Dear Nina also enjoyed teasing. She once lighted on Charlie. He was an older gentleman who frequented the bus in those early days. His personal hygiene was questionable; chips could be fried on his trousers, yet despite this we loved old Charlie.

One evening he began to bemoan the fact that he needed a good woman to look after him. "Hear that, Nina?" teased Geoff. "Charlie could do with a woman to look after him!"

"I'll look after him," offered Nina, and without further ado grabbed the startled Charlie under his arm and began taking him, protesting, up the road. Geoff had to go and rescue Charlie from this mock kidnapping because once more, my head was in the cupboard.

The flat we visited one evening was very overcrowded. There were neat stacks of books, irons, toasters, bedding, newspapers, ornaments, clothes – a whole variety of objects in a small top floor flat, in every room, and in a very narrow hallway. And that day that narrow hallway also contained Nina, in all her buxom presence. As we attempted to shuffle sideways along the length of the hall walls, we noticed Nina inching her way in the opposite direction. Geoff and I nipped into the lounge quickly, but Jason, our delicately disposed volunteer, was not so nimble. Soon Nina was standing across the hall from him in very close proximity. Jason, not knowing where to put himself, froze to the spot as Nina leaned forward from the waist – her sole purpose to make physical contact with this mortified young man.

Incidents such as these were not uncommon with lots of the needy in the early days. Usually it was we women who the men came on to. Geoff and the male volunteers protected us, of course, but, on the whole, it was myself and the women volunteers who had to bear the brunt of this harassment, until the ground rules were set out. Nowadays it is very rare. I'm afraid I was amused when Nina turned the tables on the men. Un-Christian of me, I know.

Of course, no human being should be living in Ethel's house, but Ethel, being very strong-willed, had refused to be re-housed to an old people's home. Once I got to know Ethel, I considered that this would not have been appropriate for her, and worked alongside the housing authorities, managing to move Ethel to a local sheltered accommodation, where she would have the independence of her own flat alongside the security of a warden-run establishment, and communal facilities. The move took place in the April of that first year – a wonderful opportunity, except for the fact that Ethel's old, flea-infested furniture and possessions were moved with her!

Armed with flea spray secreted up their jumpers, so as not to alarm the other residents, we and a lady volunteer named Jackie, went to settle Ethel into her new home. To our horror and amazement, we saw one of Ethel's bags wriggling; sounds of scurrying were heard from one of her cupboards! Geoff - ever the practical joker - launched his shoe onto the bed, feigning an attack on an unwelcome visitor. Poor Jackie screamed and scrammed. The thought of vermin on the bed as well as in Ethel's belongings was too much for her!

The following evening, we returned with another volunteer called James. Their task this time was to remove Ethel's infested bed. Trying not to upset the residents, I covered the bed with an old curtain, then Geoff, James and I had to take the offending article from the top floor of the building down to the waiting mission bus via a very small lift. James was not keen on anything unclean, and was trying very hard not to come into close contact with the bed – not an easy task given the close proximity! We then needed to carry it from the lift, through the building and out into the street, without anyone spying us and guessing what we were moving. Stealthily we tiptoed, casting our eyes left and right in order to avoid being seen!

In the same manner, everything from Ethel's new home had to be removed and destroyed. New items had to be found for her to make her flat into a home so different from the hovel she had come from. Funds were made available for Ethel, which I thought could be used to send her on a holiday. But Ethel had other ideas! She was too frightened to leave the security of her new home, but chose instead to have a new, bright red carpet. When it had been laid, Ethel would stand gazing at it, entranced and thrilled by her new acquisition. Her face would beam out her delight, before her eyes strayed once again to the vivid floor covering. This tiny, toothless, frail lady had come home.

Yet Ethel was still in great need of regular care – a task taken on board by Geoff and myself on a daily basis. Ethel's clothes and bedding needed washing daily since Ethel was doubly incontinent. The old lady also smoked heavily, so everything hung with the smell of cigarette smoke. My duties were not pleasant. At first Netta and I used to soak the offending articles in a bucket, before taking them home to be washed in our own washing machine. Later we made use of the facilities in the communal laundry at the complex; first soaking in the big Belfast sink then washing in the washing machine.

On one particular occasion, Geoff and Jason (the volunteer with the sensitive disposition) decided that they could take on the task of washing Ethel's things. After all, how difficult could it be to perform such an everyday task? So, having stripped the bed and having gathered Ethel's dirty clothes from me, Geoff and Jason made their way, in a determined fashion, to the laundry room – I observing wryly from a short distance. The front-loading washing machine awaited as the undomesticated gentlemen contemplated how they were going to move the soiled garments from the bucket into its drum. Whilst Geoff stood, realisation dawned that he was going to have to handle these items, and Jason stood with his head out of the window – the foulness of the bucket having pervaded the air! Not to be deterred, the two men put plan 'B' into operation! Taking hold of two mop stales like giant chopsticks, Geoff pincered the washing from the bucket into the machine, so as not to have to touch it. With a sigh of relief, he shut the door, a smile of triumph on his face. So far, so good! BUT, as Geoff stared incredulously, he spied, stuck to the transparent door of the machine, a pair of very soiled pants. In his eagerness to complete this task independently he had not asked for advice about how best to go about dealing with the obvious problems. Still, with the clothes now inside the machine, surely it would now do its best. It was then that Geoff discovered the little plastic ball. "What's this for?" he asked me. I had to straighten up and stop laughing.

"You put washing powder in it," was the amused reply.

"Then what do you do with it?"

"Well, it has to go inside the washing machine." Comprehension enlightened the faces of the two men; the washing machine door was opened at arm's length, the powder ball thrust unceremoniously in amidst the washing, before they scarpered to the safety of the land beyond the laundry room!

The unfortunate Geoff found himself to be the victim of other inanimate objects whilst caring for Ethel. Geoff – the anti-smoking Geoff; the Geoff who used to prick his mother's cigarettes with pins so that she could not suck the offending fumes – found himself with the task of having to remove furniture from the flat of this chain-smoking dependant, whenever her belongings became saturated with unpleasant odours or stains. Once, having delivered a settee which had been donated, he needed to remove the old one. He put it inside the tiny lift, closed the door, and pressed the button, only to discover that the lift had broken down. He was imprisoned in this tiny space with a sofa that was exploding cigarette fumes and ash! He was beginning to realise that when you do God's work it is important to have a sense of humour!

Gunner was another of Ethel's housemates in her previous rooms. He stayed on in that horrendous place for a while before moving to a condemned property in another area of the town. When we heard about this, we visited his new home with a mattress to replace the carpets that were proving a makeshift bed and we were able to give him blankets and food, to go with the mattress – now propped from underneath at one end with a discarded wheel serving as a pillow. Eventually, Gunner was housed in a flat of his own – one that he has kept for well over ten years, and that has played a significant part in enabling him to cut down on his drinking; for Gunner would drink anything that contained alcohol. His new home was a sanctuary that he kept free of other alcoholics.

An ex-Royal Marine, Gunner was the victim of gas and experimental warfare. His twelve year navy career made him an invalid; it also institutionalised him. He was used to having uniform, food and housing provided, and found it impossible to cope when he was released on medical grounds from his commission. He could not budget his sickness pay, and would turn to drink for solace. He soon found himself in debt, and out on the streets.

When we first encountered Gunner, he would sometimes have had his medication altered, resulting in him being "spaced out" and prone to talking in a stream of seemingly mindless nonsense. However, it soon became apparent that Gunner could use this mannerism as a way of avoiding unwelcome contact with others. No one wanted to go anywhere near this hefty figure when he was rambling. He cut too scary a picture. His size and mop of fiery hair made him look intimidating, and indeed he was a very strong man. Most of the time he would ignore unwanted approaches from others, but if they were to persist, his response was to lift the offending nuisance into the air and launch them to a distance. Yet we earned his trust in those early years; he could be left to "guard" the bus if ever Geoff was needed to go elsewhere leaving me running things for a while. Gunner would then stand hands on hips – a visible sign to potential troublemakers that these were his friends and he was there to protect them. No one messed with Gunner!

Gunner's children disowned their father when he drank to excess. Since he has had the flat, and his drinking habits have been curbed they have rekindled their relationship, keeping in touch, and visiting each other occasionally.

He used to be a formidable sight in the town, choosing to sit and drink openly anywhere in the town, both day and night. Now he can still be seen, but there is a difference: there is an absence of a can or bottle next to him. All those years ago, Gunner was banned from the pubs in the town. Now he is served, because he will drink just a couple of pints before leaving to go about his business peacefully. He is still an occasional visitor to the bus, taking only what he needs at the time. He is clean and polite and sober. Praise God for His mercies.

"Praise ye the Lord. O give thanks unto the Lord for He is good for His mercies endureth forever." Psalm 106

How easy it would have been to give up on someone like this and to say that he deserves all he gets. But we know God's mercy does endure forever, and He never gives up on us. He never gives up on anyone. Praise Him.

Chapter 6

Meeting the Need – from the back of a bus

So this is me, David; aching feet; straps from my backpack digging into my shoulders. I'm cold. The last time I ate was . . . When *was* the last time I ate? How did I get myself into this mess? What did I do wrong? When it was just me and Dad we were fine. But now this new woman's on the scene. She doesn't like me. Is it me or is it her that causes all those rows? All that shouting. All that mud slinging. And Dad always takes her side – always believes her above me. And now I'm slung out on my ear. Now where do I go? And it's all because of *her*. Why can't he see her for what she is? Why won't he believe me, and throw her out instead. It was all right before *she* came. She muscles her way into our house and thinks she can take my mum's place – bossing me about. Who does she think she is? Didn't want to live there anyway – not with her there.

I went to the library here in Leamington to get warm. I met a bloke in there, same as me: backpack, hadn't washed for days, lonely look in his eye. We got chatting and I was telling him what had happened – about that woman, and how it was her fault that I had nowhere to go. He told me that I could get some food from down the Jephson from those do-gooder Christians. He said to just look for them white buses about 6 o'clock-ish. "You get good food down there," he said, "and there's always plenty to eat. They don't ask questions and it's all free."

So I went. And he was right. I had some really nice hot soup and sandwiches. I even had a prawn sandwich – imagine! I had umpteen cups of tea, some well nice cakes – even cream ones – and home-made cookies. A bloke – I think he runs it with his wife - even gave me a bag of goodies to eat the next day.

At first I found it really hard to go down there. It's like I was a beggar. I could have cried. Is this what my life had come to, having to come down to a soup bus? And I needn't have worried, because everyone down there was friendly. I didn't feel bad at all having to ask for handouts like that. And there were loads there like me. I reckon there were about fifty of us, all ages; some sitting on the bus, some on the bench outside, and some standing around.

People in white sweatshirts, with a cross on it took round loads of food on trays; they were polite and smiled a lot. For the first time in ages I heard laughter. I saw this bloke – I think his name's Geoff – giving out blankets and sleeping bags, and I wondered how I could get one. Geoff took me to one side and asked me my name, and if I was sleeping rough. I couldn't believe it! He gave me some blankets. I won't be as cold tonight. And I'm stuffed with all that grub. For the first time in days I feel like a human being. All these people down here accepted me, without judging me. They seemed to care about what was going to happen to me. I felt that I could talk to someone who would know what I was going through.

*****

1991 we continued to walk and search for those in need during the first six months of launching the Mission. Then a friend of ours felt it right to provide the funds for us to buy a bus that would become a base for our street work, so that the needy could come to us, rather than us trudging round looking for them. We were offered three thousand pounds to buy a vehicle. It felt very strange to be offered so much money, and we said "thank you" but please could we have just half of it! Eventually we found an old social services ambulance, which was considered by some to be no more than a "rust bucket"! Nevertheless the bus was purchased, for a grand sum of seven hundred and fifty pounds. Geoff converted it into a self-contained kitchen-diner. The old fixtures and fittings were stripped out; a camping gas stove was installed; kitchen cupboards and pumped water and sink were fitted. A kitchen counter was built to divide off the preparation area from the seating area – the latter consisting of two benches. Geoff hand painted the outside of the bus white, and "Leamington Christian Mission", "Love in Action" and "Meeting the Need" was chosen by Geoff and sign-written in blue.

This was the first appearance of what is now a very familiar sight in the town. Geoff was keen to preserve the dignity of those who visited the bus. He wanted the new bus and the accompanying slogans to banish the idea of this being akin to a Victorian soup kitchen. The buses, to this day, symbolise how love in action continues to meet the needs of so many in Royal Leamington Spa. Similarly, the white sweatshirts, with the same dark blue logo single out the people who work for the Mission in many different roles.

*****

"Oh, Geoff! It's eleven o'clock and we've got to go back out again."

"Let me get in the door first! What's up?"

"Well our Bronte's had a phone call while we were down the buses. A pub landlord says he's got loads of food left from a function. We need to collect it tonight."

"What, now? What's he got then?"

"Don't ask me what he's got! Let's just go!" Could you believe it? Large catering saucepans filled to the brim with stew. Too heavy for me to hold. I had to balance them on the work surface of the bus. Did Geoff take the corners carefully? Did he not! So I ended up wearing the stuff. Sensible idea these white sweatshirts. Thank God for a sense of humour, and His bountiful supply!

How wonderful! The families we deliver these meals to are always aware of God's love for them through such provision. How practical is God's love! The truths of the Bible become real in such situations:

"What good is it, my brothers, if a man claims to have faith but has no deeds? Can such faith save him? Suppose a brother or sister is without clothes and daily food. If one of you say to him, "Go, I wish you well, keep warm and well fed," but does nothing about his physical needs, what good is it? In the same way, faith by itself, if it is not accompanied by actions is dead." (James 2 14-17)

God did not stop there. He led a man to visit the bus, from one of the leading stores in town, who asked if we would like to collect the food wastage from them each evening. We stand back in awe at God's plan. He supplied us with a regular banquet for the ones he loves. They may look like down and outs to many, but to God they are important because they are His children. And He does not give His offspring jam and bread – no – He lays before them the very best.

"Lord, thank you for providing the food for the bus. As you know, I love carrot cake! Please could we have some on the bus?" So prayed Liz, one of our volunteers one evening as we laid before God all the concerns of that day from the buses. Hundreds of pieces of carrot cake arrived on our doorstep the very next day, and continued to come, day after day. The most delicious carrot cake I had tasted was taking over the bus! Liz had primed the well! I had to ask her to stop praying.

"Give, and it will be given to you. A good measure, pressed down, shaken together and running over, will be poured into your lap. For with the measure you use, it will be measured to you." (Luke 6, 38)

So commanded Our Lord. He never wants to stop supplying our needs. Time after time we have prayed with our volunteers for specific needs. Soup, the staple of the bus menu, was running low, and Geoff asked for prayer. Silly man! He might have known that our Father God wanted to give us what we needed. A phone call brought in hundreds of gallons of best quality soup. This kept us going for a very long time.

We'd had a busy night of helping those on the streets, when, just as we were about to drive off, a man arrived from a local public house. "Could you use some tins of baked beans?" The answer was "Yes, please!" We persuaded the volunteers that they would love to help us for a little longer, and found ourselves stretched in a human chain along the stairs, hallway, pavement and out into the bus, as our God had done it again! Boxes upon boxes of the tasty produce were man handled for much longer than just a few minutes; then had to be unloaded at the other end into the store. Thank you, Lord!

These gifts are provided on a regular basis. God has continued to supply all of our needs over the fourteen years, sometimes before we have even asked. No one has gone without.

*****

The buses are multipurpose. They are kitchen, lounge, dining room, a place to pray together, to hold small Bible studies with those from the streets; for storing food and blankets, which are needed each evening. They are also removal vans.

Another phone call sent us to a house clearance. We went willingly. What an opportunity to set up house with much needed furniture and equipment for those who had been housed recently by the council.

We arrived to find that the flat to be cleared was on the third floor. There was no lift. Everything had to be sorted and packed. At that time we had the original soup kitchen bus, meaning that space was limited. Geoff lowered the tail-lift to the bus, and placed on it the three-piece suite, tying it on so that the settee was protruding about two feet. This meant that I had to sit on top of the kitchen units inside the bus and cling on to the furniture. My arms were outstretched, my feet pressed firmly to support myself. Chuckling, I reminded God that He had not shown me this in His vision! It's a good job that He and I share a sense of humour!

Over the years, hundreds of households have benefited from the supply of household goods and furniture; another example of how God gives. And as He gives us freely, so we can give to others.

*****

We were given permission to set up and serve each evening in the curved recess before the grand front gates of the esteemed Jephson Gardens in Royal Leamington Spa. For ten years those white buses

34

bore witness to the Lord's work. Talk about a party in the park - nothing but the best for God's guests – best food, best location and best love.

The bus became an essential part of the work we did – and still do. Before long it became clear that we needed another bus: one to serve from, and one to seat the growing numbers of visitors to Jephson Gardens each evening. As the years have rolled on, we have given away our faithful original bus to a local church and bought a third bus to replace it. Eventually, we were spending so much time and money in repairing and maintaining our old bus, that it became clear we needed an updated version. We prayed. "I believe that we are going to have a new bus, Geoff."

"Don't be silly. Do you realise how much these things cost?"

I answered honestly: "No, I haven't a clue. I don't do vehicles. I'm sorry, but that is what I think, and I really believe, that by this time next year we will have a brand new bus."

"No way. We will never afford the tens of thousands of pounds needed for such a vehicle."

"Okay. Well, I know that God has set aside one year. So what if we open a bank account as a bus fund, and use whatever is in that account after one year to buy whatever that amount can afford?" The deal was done. The vision was to be tested.

Very soon after that conversation, we were leading a meeting at a local church when we were approached and asked if God had given us something to do. When I replied that he had, this gentleman revealed that he had been instructed by God to give us some money. This was the first contribution to our "Bus fund". Then a local Christian businessman contacted us with the news that he was going to run the London marathon and donate the sponsorship money to the Mission. He wondered if there was a particular project that we wanted the money for. "Yes please – the bus fund!" A company in Birmingham rang and committed £2000 to the bus fund. A phone call from America could have knocked me over with a feather: "God has told me that you need a new bus. How much do you need?"

Local churches began to pledge regular amounts that went into the bus fund.

One particular church set aside an amount annually for a charity, which, traditionally had been abroad. On this occasion they had decided to make their gift to a local charity, and wondered if we would like to go and be interviewed by a team in their fellowship so that they could decide whether or not Leamington Christian Mission was the right place to send their funds. What a daunting prospect! Nevertheless, I gave the interview to God, knowing that if this bus fund was His idea then He was in control. Needless to say, the bus fund was added to as a result of that meeting!

When twelve months had been reached, the "Bus fund" had enough in it to buy the most perfect brand new Mercedes 8.1.4D van, to insure it and to run it for well over the next year. Why do we ever doubt? If we can only be the instruments for God's ideas ALL things are possible! Hallelujah!

"God spoke to me." This can be such a glib pronouncement. I have wondered when I've had it said to me of the validity of the "truths" spoken in God's name. And before Netta told me of my dream I thought I sometimes heard His voice, but after my dear friend confirmed what I had been shown I knew what I heard, or saw, accompanied by a feeling that bowls me over. I shake inside as I think of it. After all, I am not special in terms of my being very intelligent, or good. In the vastness of His hands, and the smallness of my ant-like existence, how important am I that my great and glorious Maker should want to talk to me! I know my name is written in the book of life, but I have doubts just like any other Christian from time to time, and I really do not feel worthy enough for God to use me or speak to me. Yet I have come to recognise His call; to implement His wishes; to know that His schemes are daring, scary and fruitful! A Christian should never be classed as a wimp – not if they are in dialogue with the Almighty – because from my experience, He sets us on a course that requires guts and determination akin to that needed by the most intrepid explorer. We don't travel lightly, though. We are equipped with a huge amount of faith given to us for the journey. I certainly did not have such faith before the vision for the Mission was revealed. But since then, I rest peacefully when God asks us to do something, or reveals His latest project, because I know that He is in charge. Yes, we carry out operations, but He steers the ship. The boat and its crew are in His care. So if it is to be, it will be, if I let go and let God, and stop wanting to take over the proceedings!

We serve many different people at the buses, with many different needs and temperaments. Whilst most are compliant and grateful, there are some who are drug and alcohol dependant, and who have been known to be violent towards us.

"What do you reckon you're doing? What are you doing all this for? You're do gooders. You'll only do this work for five minutes. You don't really care about us. What are you doing? Are you getting millions out of looking after us?"

"We're doing this to share God's love with you."

"God doesn't want to know me! I belong to the Devil!"

So we were challenged with this and many other similar conversations with the ones we helped at the buses. Yet God also heard these conversations and by His grace turned the situation around.

About ten minutes into the evening service, Peter, our Pastor, nodded to us to go to the back of the church. As we turned, we saw four visitors – not ones we would normally expect to see in any church! They were the ones we met with at the buses; heavily clad in layers of dark clothing, unkempt and carrying their unique dusty, musty, smoky aroma. We asked them to come in, and we sat with them at the back of the building, where they preferred to be. They had come to see where we were coming from. But these people were unchurched. They did not follow the etiquette expected from regular church attendees. They muttered and mumbled, questioning aspects of the meeting, not in hushed tones, but in a normal talking voice. They were searching for answers, but managed to disrupt the meeting in so doing. Over time there were many from the buses who joined us at church meetings. Some stayed and some drifted away.

Our church members had to endure more than just interruptions to the services on occasions. When a few of us were chatting at the end of one meeting, we were surprised, then shocked, then afraid when four men from the buses came into the building, and one of them began waving a hand gun. He and his friends were inebriated. The young man with the gun flailed the weapon, abuse issuing from his mouth. Our sisters and brothers in Christ took flight amidst screams and cries of fear. Yet I did not feel afraid. "Come on now. Stop being so silly. What do you think will happen to you if you are caught with that thing? Give it to me, please, and go." Where did I get such an assurance of safety? For that is what it was. It was not bravery, not foolishness that led me to approach him. I just knew that he was not seriously intending to use the gun. I just *knew!* Praise Him who knew before I did! Needless to say, the man put the gun in his pocket and left the building. I was left to soothe the nerves of church members.

We have often been asked to pray with people as we minister on the street. When Graham asked Geoff to pray for him one evening at the buses, Geoff was blessed with a word of knowledge. God was asking Graham to return to Wales to tend to his daughter. Graham was amazed. How did Geoff know about his child? *No one* had been told about her. Graham balked then acted. He listened and obeyed God, setting his affairs in order. Some time later he came to church, and when the call came to go forward, Graham stepped to the altar and made a commitment.

When my friend Netta saw how Graham had responded to the Word, God witnessed to her spirit that she should come and help us at the buses. In those days she would start at four o'clock and work on a voluntary basis for six hours twice a week.

Graham was moved and convicted by God speaking directly into his life. He became protective of us. He behaved towards us as children of God and that the place in which we stood was holy.

*****

There are many different aspects to our work. We meet many different people – some of them remarkable.

Part of our work involves sharing God and how He uses us. We were asked to speak in a church in Warwick. There we met a young girl of fourteen years, called Martha, and were impressed by her caring nature and her mature outlook. She had organized and led her youth group. There were about twenty youngsters in the group, many of them older than her. After hearing our talk, she felt moved by the plight of the homeless, and organized a sleep out for the young people. Trying to mimic the ones who slept rough, they took cardboard, blankets, pillows and teddy bears and stayed outside overnight in the church gardens. They asked people to sponsor them, and gave the proceeds to the Mission.

Over the next year we kept in touch with her. She so desperately wanted to help us as a volunteer, which was impossible because of her age. At the end of the year, we had a phone call from one of the secondary schools in the area, asking if we would take a young girl on work experience, as this person wanted to gain experience that may be of use to her in a possible career as a social worker. We were surprised and pleased to discover that this was the same girl who, twelve months earlier had organised the sleep out.

The work experience required her to see and become involved in all aspects of our work, over the course of a week. This meant that she worked down at the store, sorting clothes, putting food away, preparing food for the buses, addressing envelopes, folding and stuffing the newsletter, prayer letter and needs letter in the envelopes. She shadowed me for the whole week. Thursday morning there were Christmas presents to wrap, and this was only February! I explained to her that there were over five thousand to wrap, and it cannot be left to the end of the year. Thursday afternoon, food hampers were prepared for the families. These were the families who were very poor, for various reasons, and needed food for the children for the weekend. Friday afternoon I took her with me to deliver these hampers. She was surprised because it involved more than just delivering food. Many of them had problems that they needed to discuss with me. There were others who could not read; who may have had a letter to sort out. Others would need help sorting out their finances, so that their bills might be paid.

As we travelled from one house to the next we had opportunity to talk. She began asking me questions about my faith. I shared with her how I became a Christian, and how it had changed my life. We discussed the truths of the Bible. She contemplated on what we had spoken of, and then said: "I'm not sure I believe all of the Bible. I know some of it's true, but it doesn't all make sense."

"You don't have to believe me," I replied. "When you go to bed tonight just pray that God will speak to you and show you that it is all true. And He will reveal His truth."

The following night began as usual. Then trouble brewed as Bridie was on the bus, drunk and ready for a fight. She had had a row with her boyfriend and was in no mood to cooperate. Bridie, the Bag Lady (I say a lady loosely), had lived on the streets for most of her life. She was in her early sixties, although her weather-beaten face and general demeanor were deceptive. She had a son and a daughter. We later met her son, who had been in prison for knee-capping a man for raping his sister. Whilst in prison he had given his life to Christ, and his life had changed. We later found him accommodation, but he had lived on the streets for so long that he found it very difficult to live with a roof over his head. So he gave up his flat and moved on. We heard eighteen months later that he had been found dead in an alley.

We first encountered Bridie on the steps of the Parish church in Leamington. She had a blanket around her shoulders. Her hair fell in straggly tendrils framing her face with matted tangles. She portrayed an image of helplessness and poverty. We wondered how society could abandon such a frail old person to the harsh elements. This could be someone's little granny – or so we thought. As we approached her she gave us a sob story, and asked for money. She said that she needed the money for the train fare to Ireland. (It is the Mission policy never to give money, as we would have a queue miles long each evening.) We offered to buy her a meal, or provide her with her needs, but this was not what she wanted. The real Bridie was then revealed. She began to abuse us verbally. Later we discovered how she would carry a broken bottle and a knife to defend herself. We could never turn our back on her.

40

*****

Bridie had a young man friend who would be there for her. He also had lots of problems, he was an alcoholic, a drug user, and had associated health problems. They were a sight to behold!

Irony surrounds Bridie like the dirty blanket she wrapped around herself. The pitch in which one of the volunteers was collecting money for Leamington Christian Mission was also occupied by our bag lady. Any thought of sharing this church porch way was abhorrent to her. She told our volunteer in no uncertain terms to shift out of the way; that this was her pitch and she was there first! She was worried that when the people came out of church, that the volunteer would claim any offerings and she would lose out! . . .

"What are we going to do tonight? We've been chucked out from that shop doorway; wasn't our fault the bloomin' thing set on fire! It was nice and sheltered in there as well. Now look at us, we're out on our ear again. They keep movin' us on. We're goin' to have to find somewhere of our own that they can't move us from. They won't give us a bloomin' flat. I saw an old caravan in that field. We could use that if we could get someone to move it for us. You know that old feller who gets in the way at that church? I reckon I could get round him – he's always helpin' folk out. I'd bet he'd do it! He wouldn't want to see us on the streets . . ."

"What're we goin' to do now? That fire's took the bloomin' roof off this caravan. Look now: the bloomin' weather's changed and it's tiddling down. I reckon we'll 'ave to get round that feller again; see what he'll come up with. It was no bovver, this caravan. It's a shame." . . .

When her roofless caravan finally lost its tarpaulin cover, Bridie was forced to camp out in another place. Being who she was, she chose the car park of the local council offices. They soon found her a home . . . "This place is all right since I told that old boy to get us some furniture. It wasn't much cop without. It's handy too, being

41

right next to the pub! Kind of the council to sort that out for us. Only problem is, these nosey gits keep staring at us through the window. One of these days I'll sort them out."

On the night in question Bridie was furious because she had seen her man friend go off with a woman of ill repute. Bridie was therefore angry with anyone she came into contact with. Geoff especially was a target. As he entered the bus with a flask of soup she was verbally offensive, so he asked her politely to leave the bus and sit outside. Without warning her feet and fists began flailing towards Geoff, catching others in their wake. When any similar trouble occurs, we ask the volunteers to step aside, leaving Geoff and myself to deal with the matter. I stepped out of the kitchen bus to help Geoff to persuade Bridie, with patience and reason from the other bus. She took some persuasion and had to be removed for the safety of the others on the bus. I never turn my back on the ones we help, but for some reason I did this particular time, and Bridie saw her chance for retribution and took advantage of the situation. Reaching out, she grabbed a large chunk of my hair and held fast. She was determined not to let go. Three male volunteers tried to get her to release me, but without success. She only let go as she ripped her huge prize painfully from the crown of my head. I took one look at her hands and saw a mass of hair. It was a mass of *my hair!* At this point my thoughts were not Christian ones! I ran onto the bus and asked the volunteers "Please, please pray for me! I should not be thinking what I am thinking at this moment!"

As I considered my locks in the hands of this deranged woman, my vanity foresaw a bald spot right in the middle of my head. God still has work to do on me! It was very painful. My head was hurting. As they prayed for me I felt God's peace and felt I could go outside amongst the needy, and face Bridie again as she sat by the gate, oblivious to the chaos she had caused. She was eating her sandwich and drinking her soup with calm indifference.

Amidst all the clamour and pain I was surprised to hear a little voice saying "I now believe in the whole Bible, and that God is real." I turned around and saw Martha – realisation on her young

42

face. "Thank you very much Lord, but be aware that I am not amused. There is only so much hair on my head." Then I looked at Martha and realised that she was worth it; then I laughed.

Bridie is still living on the streets. She is still drinking and roaming from place to place, but stays in Leamington most of the time. She has been in prison for arson and grievous bodily harm. Yet there is something vulnerable about her, something that makes us want to continue to help her.

"There's a man threatening to throw himself off the bridge! Can anyone help?" Then the lady disappeared! Geoff looked at me. I looked at Geoff. We looked at Mark.
"You'll have to manage!" And off Geoff ran, leaving me and Mark to serve the hungry dozens outside the Jephson Gardens.

Geoff found the man on the river side of the bridge over the river Leam. "Get lost you do gooder! I'm going to jump!"
"You won't do it there, mate! The water's not deep enough. But you could break your legs, or die from pollution!" Without more ado, the man launched himself off the bridge. Geoff made a grab for his wrist, and in so doing was pulled with his belly over the top of the bridge. Geoff's legs were off the floor and searching desperately for a foothold onto the pillars of the bridge sides. "Can anybody help me? This bloke's going to fall. I can't hold him much longer!" To his dismay, for a while no one stopped to help the dangling Geoff. Eventually, a kind passer-by (the Good Samaritan) helped Geoff to yank the unhappy man from his thwarted suicide attempt. The two rescuers frog-marched him to the red public telephone boxes and 'persuaded' him to wait in there until the police arrived. All the while he was pushing and kicking against the heavy door in an effort to escape his well-meaning rescuers.

In the meantime, at the buses, 'the Crazy Man' was causing trouble, which meant that no one from our team was able to go and help Geoff on the bridge. When the police had escorted the bridge jumper away, Geoff returned and wondered what on earth was going on, until he spotted Crazy Cedric drunk and disorderly as usual!

Geoff knew instantly where the trouble lay, and in view of his recent ordeal, threw his Christian patience to the wind and dealt with Cedric in no uncertain terms, telling him to go or be banned from the buses. Cedric was being violent in his drunken state, and would not listen to reason.

We had started out that summer's evening thinking that it would be just another ordinary soup run; little did we know! God enables us to do the unusual. With His help it all worked out. Thank God that man did not lose his life. We started laughing as we prayed. What next. Lord? We could have a peaceful life. We could be sitting at home, watching the television. But that is not for us. This is the life for us. God knows me better than I know myself.

*****

"How can these people call themselves Christians when they won't give me any food! I'm bloomin' starvin'. If they had given me what I wanted I wouldn't have pulled that knife! They make me sick. If it wasn't for the likes of us they wouldn't be millionaires. It's 'cause of us they've got all this money. It must cost them thousands to feed all these folk every night, and pay for them buses. And they get all that furniture and other stuff to set us all up. They've got to have got the money from somewhere. I mean, that night they paid for me and George and Gill and Steve to stay in that hostel. It must have cost a packet. They'll never give us any money though. They're just tight beggars!"

"I can't even go up on a Thursday any more to get that money off Ethel when she gets her pension. That Steph has taken her book; she looks after her money, now. It was a real good earner that was. It used to pay for all our drinks for a couple of nights. Why couldn't that interfering woman leave it alone. I'm going to have a word with Dick. He'll sort 'em out for me when I tell him what they've done. I'm still hungry, but I'm blowed if I'm going to apologise so that I can go back on that bus! Who's here that I could ask to get me some? Geoff doesn't have to know it's for me. Mind you, I tried that last time I was banned and that nosey woman came out and snatched that butty straight out of my hand! You can't get away with a bloomin' thing down here. She's eyes in the back of her head!"

*****

You might think that the buses are no place for children, but over the years we have seen hundreds of hungry children brought down to the buses. Those cups of soup and handfuls of sandwiches may have been the only meal of the day.

One evening a father and his two children came along to be fed. There was a boy and a girl of about five and six years old. They were both very dirty. They were living on a canal boat. They did not go to school – their father did not see the point. He had not been himself, and, as he said, he was all right; he had managed. We gave them food and clothing for the children and their parents. We also handed out other things such as candles, razors, soap and shampoo. However, when we offered the father some soap, he refused it, saying: "I have better things to do with water than wash!" These children had not had a proper wash and had never been to school. The authorities could not catch up with them as they moved from one mooring place to another. We would wonder how they could survive. Yet they did, in their own way.

These boat children would sit by the pavement when they came to the buses. They were never any trouble. Our hearts went out to them. Was this the life they would always have? Yet their father loved them and in his way he was doing the best he knew how. We are arrogant enough to think that we know best about how a child should be brought up. But who are we to stand in judgement over these parents? Isn't loving the most important thing – the basis of any relationship. A child cannot develop without it.

"Why don't you scroungers go out and get a job? Try looking after yourselves for a change, instead expecting everyone else to do it for you."

This is the viewpoint of some people. (Only a few.) We have heard the taunts. Yet we do not always know the reasons why these folks are in such a predicament.

We are always asked whose fault it is when young people are homeless. Is it the parents; could it be the schools and their lack of discipline; is there no discipline in the homes? How can so many young people have no future? What drives them to take drugs? Why do they turn to drink, end up shoplifting? We do not have the answers to these questions – we can only come alongside them and try to turn them back on track. We are asked if they have come from bad families. Have they been brought up in poverty? Do they have parents who are on drugs, or dependant on alcohol? And to all of these questions we could answer "Yes". Some have come from broken families. Some have come from households where their parents are dependant on drugs and alcohol. We may recognize that this is so in some cases, but some do come from respectable families, who have just been led into substance abuse. There are those, who through no fault of their own find themselves homeless.

William, James and Peter – all brothers, the eldest being seventeen - were being brought up by their widowed mother. Her sons were a credit to her. None of them had been in trouble of any sort. They had all finished their full time education. But there came a time when their mother met and fell in love with a man, and was happy because at last she had someone looking after her. It was her time now to be looked after. She had needs of her own. The man asked her to marry him, but there was a condition attached – he wanted her but not the boys. After soul-searching she chose the man, and the boys were asked to leave the home. Unfortunately, being the age that they were, they were not eligible to sign for accommodation on their own behalf. Therefore, they were homeless. It was not long before they had no money, and found themselves down at the bus.

They were homeless with no money for a flat. Without a home it is hard to find employment.

Whose fault was this? So often we judge young people. But we do not know how they came to be in the position they are in. We do not know what life has thrown at them. We need to walk a mile in their shoes.

Chapter 7

Let us Sow Seeds and See Fruit

Oh Lord, I know you have called me to sow seeds for you, but my heart is longing to see fruit. Please, one day let me see people coming to salvation. I know that when we sow seeds you will bring someone forward to water them, and then someone to harvest. I want to be present at the reaping.

"Hear my cry, Oh Lord. Attend to my prayer. From the ends of the Earth I will cry to you, when my heart is overwhelmed. Lead me to the rock that is higher than I .For you have been a shelter to me ,A strong tower from the enemy." Psalm 61 v1 New King James

My heart was crying out to God. The work was so hard at times. Day after day we watched people destroying their lives. We pray for them, but we do not always see the change that is needed to turn their lives around, and I longed to see God's hand on their lives. So I cried out: "Please, Lord, bless this work! I know this work is yours. I have to be patient and watch your hand at work, but it is so hard at times. Susan and others have taken a large part of me. And yet, Lord I wonder how long I have got to wait before I see even a shoot coming up, let alone the fruit? Please, Lord, let us sow seeds and see fruit." God is a listening ear to all we say. We so often try to work God's plan out, but He has a plan for our lives. We need to wait; to be patient; to stand in awe of what God can do. He had heard my plea. He was to send encouragement by the caravan load!

One Sunday evening, in 1993, we came across sixteen strangers sitting quietly at the back of our church. As we drank tea after the service, Geoff and I chatted to them, and discovered that they were Romany gypsies who had just moved into the area. As the conversation progressed we were invited to visit them. So, the following Thursday evening after the soup run, we went to their site. As we arrived we were greeted with such enthusiasm. They all came running across the field to welcome us, as if we were long-lost friends. They were so eager to have us sit with them in their caravan. We were served tea in the most beautiful bone china cups; they were to be washed up in a lead crystal bowl. We sat on sofas protected by plastic covering. Everywhere was spick and span. With no mains water, and amidst a muddy field, it felt as if we were in a palace. These people were so proud of their homes and their heritage. Here was a whole family of Romanies – an extended family spanning generations. They lived according to age-old traditions of Romany gypsies. They spoke of the respect and care they had of each other. They told us of the tree-felling jobs they carried out from town to town.

The conversation turned to God. "Please pray for us. We need to be saved!" At that twenty people fell on their knees on the caravan floor, followed by Geoff, Vernal and myself. The Holy Spirit swept over us all. An uncontrollable force heralded the presence of God – a most amazing feeling! I did not know whether to laugh or cry. We laid hands on each person and prayed.

When we finally got up off our knees and continued talking they shared how they had listened to the whole Bible – in two days! They could not read well enough to read the Bible, so they went to the Christian bookshop and bought it on tape. They told us that God was calling the gypsies.

"It says in the Bible: 'Go into the highways and byways and bring them in.' That's us! We're the ones in the byways." It was incredible to us how God had witnessed to them through His word. We can read the Bible for years and yet not hear what God has to say to us. Yet in two days, these new friends had not only listened but they had acted on His word. We became close, and continued to visit them. Again they threw at us a task that made us smile. They had been listening again!

"Go ye in the name of the Lord and be baptized." They wanted to follow in Jesus's footsteps. As we sat smiling we looked out of the window. "We need water to baptize you, and there isn't even a puddle outside." We told them that they needed to talk to our Pastor, who agreed to baptize them. What a great privilege it was to be present as they went into the water, emerging as new creations.

There came a time for them to move on. It was sad to see them go, but we kept in touch with them for a long time. They asked us to pray for the head of their family to be saved, since he was the only one out of about thirty people who had not come to the Lord. They shared how they had gone all over the country to tent campaigns with thousands of other gypsies who were Christians. They believed that God was using the simple people of this land to confound the wise. And God answered their prayer – their father (the head of the family) was saved.

God works in mysterious ways, His many wonders to perform. This experience will never leave us. I asked for one soul and He gave us thirty. God's well is always overflowing. We do limit our God. I am as guilty as the rest. We pray, but do not always expect an answer. When He does, He does to Bless us – and what a blessing we had. What a blessing these dear gypsies were. They will always be in my heart. Thank you, Lord.

*****

I shared with Nancy, one of our volunteers, about what had happened when we met the gypsies and how wonderful God was to let us be present when He led His precious ones to salvation. Nancy shared with us how she would have loved to be part of such an experience; to see the Holy Spirit fall on the caravan. She then asked that if another group came, she would love to go with us to visit them.

A few months later another group of gypsies came to the buses. This time they were parked in a field near Longbridge Island. We decided one evening to go and introduce ourselves. We invited Nancy and Netta to join us. Again, we were welcomed with open arms. We enjoyed many a cup of tea in their beautiful homes. We felt led by the Holy Spirit to visit once or twice a week. They were interested in our calling and why we were doing the work we were doing. They began questioning us about the Bible and the message of the Gospel.

Over time we became friends with these sixteen adults and their many children and lots and lots of dogs! We found out that they were Tarmacers. Their site was a very muddy field, but it was only temporary, as the farmer needed them to move on after a couple of weeks. They then moved a couple of miles up the road to Warwick, onto a piece of derelict land where they stayed for about eight weeks.

One evening we arrived to find that one of their dogs was having puppies – such a small thing, yet we were privileged to be allowed to see this arrival of new life into their community. God did answer Nancy's prayer – again we were on our knees in a caravan as these people gave their lives to the Lord. God is so gracious. Again He had blessed us by allowing us to be reapers of fruit, not just sowers. For so long we had sown seeds for God, not knowing if they grew. But here we had, once more, seen fruition.

Whilst they stayed in our locality we were able to teach the children about the love of God. Netta and Nancy brought books for the children. They sat and told them stories as they were being put to bed at the other end of the caravan. These people were also baptized, this time at a tent campaign, with hundreds of gypsies present.

When God opens doors we do not know where it will lead. One evening down at the soup bus a man came and told us that he was part of a group of travellers that was camped up the road.
"Have you got any food you can spare?"
"How many of you are there, mate?" asked Geoff. "Tell them to come down to the bus, and we'll feed them."
"There's about twenty of us, but they won't want to come here. That's why I've come down. They won't want to mix with these sorts." We told them that they were welcome to whatever food we had left at the end of the evening, and so he left, telling us where to find them.

When God gives us extra mouths to feed, He also sends the provision. Half way through that evening, unexpectedly, a food van selling hot savoury pies came and asked us if we could use a hundred of his surplus wares. God knew long before we did that these unfortunate travellers would be in need of sustenance.

We took the food to where they were parked, under the railway bridges, and left them with full stomachs. We wondered if we might be given another opportunity to feed their souls as well as their bodies, but on this occasion they did not respond. But this did not stop us. We gave them food each time they came to the buses, and tried to show them the love of God. We prayed that God would water the seeds that we had sown. They continued to come and feel welcome – and they were welcome to what we had.

This brings to mind three people who lived in a double-decker bus: a young couple and their baby. They had converted the bus by making a bedroom on the lower deck with a double bed, a wood burning stove with a chimney leading from the lower deck up through the upper deck and out of the roof. This kept both decks warm. A kitchen had been built on the lower deck. A sitting room was on the top. There were curtains at all the windows. They had made it into a proper home. They wanted to know why we wanted to help them. We shared how we had felt God had told us to help anyone in need; to show His love through our hands by feeding the poor. They were so blessed by what we had to say that the lady cried. We asked if they would like a Bible. We were pleased that they accepted and took it with them as they continued on their travels. We had to leave our bus dwellers in God's hands. This is why, when God gives us a diamond, an opportunity to be part of His wonderful plan, we hold it close to our heart as a most precious gift.

Chapter 8

Holidays

Haven't we got enough to do, Lord? Not another vision! Yes, God gave me another vision – a picture of six caravans in a row. Then, as I prayed God brought back the memory of my childhood holidays at Anderby Creek near Skegness. At that time there was a Christian group that would come to the beach in the mornings and sing of the love of God. There were games – such a lot of fun. I felt that God was showing me of how good it was to learn about Jesus.

An incident that had happened a few days before came to me as I was praying. A family with two boys – Andy aged six and Ian aged four – had a father who was an alcoholic. We visited this family regularly, providing them with food and clothing. We often had a chance to talk through their problems. On this particular evening when we arrived to the shouts of: "The Cistians are coming! The Cistians are coming!" the parents were in the middle of a violent argument. We stepped in, feeling that the children should be removed. Geoff, Pat and a male volunteer took the two boys to the soup bus, whilst Vernal and I separated the parents. The mother came with me and Vernal took the father to different parts of the house. Whilst we were talking and praying with them Geoff and Pat were talking and praying with the boys. "What would you like to be when you grow up?" asked Geoff.
"I'm going to be a Cistian!" was the enthusiastic reply.
"What do Christians do?"
"They give out veggies and food. They looks after people."

My caravan filled prayers reminded me of how people such as these had a good experience of Christians, but that their understanding of what it was to be a Christian had poor foundations. They enjoyed the links that they had with us as Christians, but they had not yet understood that Christ had died for them. They loved the soup without the Gospel. God showed me a room in which I was to

53

teach the children. And the theme – "What is a Christian?"

"Ok, Lord, I will trust you. I haven't a clue where to start. We haven't enough funds for this. I don't know where to take these people. I've never booked a caravan before. Where do I start? I don't know whether Geoff's going to understand!" Geoff's reaction was cautious: "I know that none of these families have ever been to the seaside before but how are we going to do all this work? Have you really thought about how much this is going to cost? Are you really going to have enough time to organize all this?"

"But God said . . ." and so Geoff gave in!

"Ok, Lord, how do I go about finding a caravan site?" Peter, our Pastor, had some practical suggestions as a starting point. I had been given a specific date – right at the most expensive part of the long summer holidays. God had given me a wish list: six eight-berth caravans in a straight row; a room in which to teach the children; the site was to be by the sea; we were to take families. My remit was not just for the children. It was to give guidance to the parents on how to approach their parenting, and to give them the opportunity to have fun together. And so I began calling many caravan parks. Since this was the busiest time of the year, and I was giving just a few weeks' notice, I was not having much joy. At the point when I was feeling despondent, because nowhere seemed to have what we needed, I telephoned a holiday park in Wales. The site owner asked me how many caravans I wanted. Taking a deep breath and steeling myself for yet another disappointment, I asked for the six, eight-berth caravans. He said he had them, but the only ones he had were brand new vans. He told me that they were in a straight line. My joy to know that God had reserved these for us. Not only had we been given the caravans, but they were the best – only the best for His people! Then I needed to ask for the room in which to do all the teaching and activities. "Yes, there is a small office you can use," he replied, "it will be £25 per session."

"I need it each morning from 9 till 12, and again from 4pm to 6.30pm on the Friday"

"OK. But who are you, and why do you need the room?"

When I told him he offered the ballroom instead, for the whole week for a grand total of £25! He also gave us £50 off each caravan! This man did not even know us, yet he was so generous, saving us over £450. This was just what we had required. We knew that this was from God. Everything that we had been shown was to be provided. This was the confirmation that God was at work in our lives. He had opened yet another door, sweeping aside the doubts and the concerns, and making us realize that we do nothing in our own strength, but in the strength of God. God had been before us, and even laid it on the heart of this man – this stranger – to give. Always trust in the Lord. He will provide your needs.

By the time the holiday came about every penny of the money had been provided. We arranged transport and collected the food together. Geoff, myself, some volunteers and five families were to travel together on this holiday of discovery.

One of our volunteers was so excited about this venture that he felt moved to buy us some baseball caps, and asked what we would like printed on the front of them. These white caps bore "Jesus is Lord" in blue writing, and were a wonderful way of identifying our party from a distance. They were to be a great witness around the site.

We were delighted, knowing that God's hand was on this holiday, and yet He had so much more in store for us. I was planning to give everyone a fish and chip tea on the Friday evening and to give the children the opportunity to show their parents all that they had learned. I wanted to follow this by a prize giving, presenting the children with a Bible. Before we left I visited the local Christian bookshop, with a sum of £6 per child as my budget. I felt it needed to be a well-illustrated version to continue the teaching that would be started on the holiday. I was shown the full Bible and the New Testament, which was ideal. I was so disappointed to find that we could only afford the New Testament. The order went in, and we were called to go and pick them up when they arrived. To our amazement, we found that the distributor had felt led to send the full Bible for the price of the New Testament. I stand in awe of what God can do. Again He confirmed that this is what He wanted us to do.

A local evangelist together with guitar and family, three volunteers, six families who had never before had a holiday together, Geoff and myself all with cars packed to bursting set off one Saturday morning in the July sunshine to Wales and the eagerly awaited holiday.

The caravans were lovely – ideal of course – with three bedrooms, a bathroom, a fully equipped kitchen and a bed settee in the lounge. They were spacious – 36 feet by 12 feet. And they were luxurious too. No one had used them before us. Our families were thrilled by their accommodation. The look on their faces is something I shall never forget. The children ran up and down the caravans, jumping on the settees in their excitement, and announced in disbelief: "We've got our own bedroom!"

Their pleasure was further compounded by the rest of the site. There was a café and a large indoor swimming pool, a ballroom for entertainment in the evening, and for our teaching sessions in the daytime. And, wonder of wonders, the beautiful sandy beach was just a ten-minute walk away.

Sunday morning all the volunteers came to our caravan for a praise and worship time. We needed to come before the Lord to prepare ourselves for the time ahead. Our first beach crusade was to follow. We all marched down to the shore wearing our "Jesus is Lord" baseball caps. The old and the young rambled expectantly towards the waves and the sand. We set down guitar, flute, huge cards containing the words of the choruses, balls, cricket bats, beach mats for sitting on and drinks, laying them in a secluded part of the beach. Nevertheless, people gathered round as we sang our choruses! The onlookers stood with amused faces as I did a realistic impression of a monkey:

"Who's the king of the jungle (ooh ooh!)
Who's the king of the sea (bubble bubble bubble)
Who's the king of the universe (arms circle)
The jungle and of me
"J-E-S-U-S is

He's the king of me
He's the king of the universe
The jungle and the sea (bubble bubble ooh ooh)."

The sun was shining. We felt the Lord's presence amongst the joyous singing and merry games on the summer sand. It was a pleasure to share our activities and worship with the other holiday-makers. Then it was back to the ballroom to paint the huge collage depicting "What is a Christian". This enormous length of paper told the story of the Gospel starting with the birth of Christ and finishing with His resurrection. We worked together on this weeklong project with the children, giving the parents a free morning. We would have quizzes to reinforce the teaching from the beach, and more choruses – of course! The children were taught memory verses in rap and sang the Lord's Prayer.

We rapped to the verse in 1Peter:

"Casting all your cares on Him because He cares for you." And, from Romans 10: *"Everyone who calls upon the name of the Lord shall be saved."*

What promises for those children to remember? A seed had been sown. Who knows when the harvest will be? For those young people are now adults, some with children of their own. I just pray that they own something of the beliefs and values offered over the time we worked with them.

Unbeknown to us, the owner of the site was watching as we enjoyed our teaching time. He asked me to go and see him. I was concerned that we had done something to upset someone, and prepared myself for a confrontation. To my surprise he asked me if I would be prepared to run a camp like this next year, and make this a regular event. You might guess what my reply was – a resounding "NO!" I think now what a wonderful opportunity this could have been, but at the time, I was acutely aware of how much time, effort and money this venture had taken. It was a good idea, but this would have been of man not of God. This holiday had happened as a result of a vision. It had been God led, and may happen again if He chose to guide me to organize another one. The site owner was so impressed and touched by what he saw, not just in the ballroom. He witnessed the good behaviour of all our guests, and the joy as they sang heartily zigzagging in-between the caravans. What a witness! These children with baseball caps at every angle announcing, "Jesus is Lord", were uninhibited, dashing from place to place as they practiced their choruses and memory verses. Other holidaymakers and even the cleaners came to the ballroom, standing at the back and listened to us teaching the children. One was so impressed that he videoed the whole morning.

One of the things that delighted us was the way in which the holiday enabled the parents to play with their children. The holiday site had a wonderful swimming complex. In the afternoons we would all meet – parents, children, volunteers, Geoff and myself – and go swimming! We had great fun playing with the water toys: leaping off the large rafts, climbing inside huge rubber rings, throwing and catching beach balls, squealing as we slid and twisted down water chutes.

We take it for granted that adults know how to be parents, and know how to play with their children. But when we watched them we saw how difficult they found it. Many of these parents had not been taught by their own parents. There was no positive role model. They mimicked how *their* parents had behaved towards them. They witnessed shouting and fights. Men and women thumped one another in the presence of these children. The children would scowl in a corner, frightened to move. They dared not speak.

I read to my children, because I was read to. I played make-believe with teddies and dolls; made dens with old sheets pegged onto clothes horses; built jigsaws; did junk modelling; painted our hands and feet in the garden; molded with play dough; teemed and ladled with water; sang with actions. But the children we took on holiday had never experienced such positive interaction with their parents because they in turn did not know how to play with their children. This holiday was a learning curve – it exposed the parents to the fun side of parenting, to the rewards of getting alongside your own children and enjoying each other's company. We trust in God – that these children will know and remember how to interact with their own children later on in life.

We do what we feel God has asked us to do, but we don't see the whole picture. God had used the meetings for the children to sow so many seeds. We may not know who waters those seeds or if they will bear fruit – we can only leave them in God's hands. This is God's plan, not ours.

On the last teatime of our holiday, we brought the families all together in the ballroom. We ordered yummy fish and chips from the chip van on the caravan site. This was a way of bringing everyone together for the children to strut their stuff in front of their parents! They made us so proud. Their parents ended up learning their songs with them.

"God loves you,
And I love you
And that's the way it should be."

One of the families that we took away had four children. These children were abused – not physically. They were subjected to mental degradation on a daily basis. The incidents were even more severe when their mother and their stepfather had been drinking.

The words of the chorus was the reassurance claimed by a little girl who, only hours before had been made to sit with her brothers and sister on the settee and told not to move. This was the faith of someone who was told regularly by her mother that she was useless, and that she was not loved. This was the comfort of a child who would frequently share one bag of chips with her brothers and sisters as their main meal. They lived in a four-bedroom house. The carpets were shiny, the pile eaten up by grease, the footfall sticky. The whole house was filthy. The back garden was like a wilderness – a mess of overgrown vegetation entangled by old furniture, bags of rubbish and broken toys. Piles of washing festered in the kitchen. Nothing was looked after; the children were not taught how. They, in turn did not know how to love or how to be loved. When we taught them the chorus: "God loves you . . ." God planted a seed in the heart of the eldest child. "Aunty Steph, when I go to bed at night, I sing that song to myself and I know that God loves me."

She went to bed with an insult instead of a cuddle. She was told that she was a horrible girl and that no one could love her. She went to bed feeling ugly and unwanted. Crying to herself, she would recall that we told her to pray, and she kept remembering the chorus. If no one else could love her, then she knew that God would love her. If only for this one girl, this holiday was worth all the hard work.

It was really very simple. We needed a caravan park geared up for families. We needed eight caravans, each big enough for a family. All the caravans needed to be in a line. We needed a room where we could have children's teaching and activities. God showed me all this, so this is what I asked for when making enquiries. And guess what? We had everything as requested! Praise Him who always knows more than we do!

It was impractical to take all the families with whom we came into contact on a week's holiday. Some of the children had never been on holiday; had never seen the seaside. So, once a year, we accompany a coach full of people to the coast – all 106 in two coach-loads!

In the early days, there were lessons to be learned to ensure the smooth running of this trip. One such instruction was given when several families set off, armed with their own food, down to Southsea. Ben, the youngest child of one of the families, looking cherub-like, bedecked in his little white and navy sailor's suit went along with his mother, father, brother and sisters. Lynne, his mother, and her friend's family began to open their picnic whilst on the journey, unscrewing the lid from a huge jar of pickled onions to have with their packups. At one point one of the pickled onions flirted from eager fingers and rolled under the seats, to be followed by a sailor-suited toddler who dived after it with great enthusiasm.

Despite the fact that the rotating morsel had collected fluff and bits of unidentifiable origin, once Ben had caught up with it he still enjoyed munching it!

Needless to say, when Ben had completed his under-seat slide, his once white attire was anything but white. Since that trip, food has been banned on the coach – everyone has to wait until their destination before having their lunch.

After the ban on food in the coach it was necessary to provide food for our many travellers. A small army of willing butterers, fillers and packers assembled the day before in my kitchen telling me "Thank you very much, but we don't need to sit down." Once the enormous tubs of margarine and the dozens of loaves of bread, scones and tea cakes were laid out for preparation, the dear ladies changed their minds and chairs were provided. Beryl arrived after everyone else and asked what she could do.

"Would you mind grating some cheese for the sandwiches?" said I. "No problem," she replied. Her facial expression changed to one of horror as she stared in disbelief at the seven pound block of cheese! She then noticed that she had only one hand grater to use. What a servant! She persevered through the entire block. Everyone had thought that this exercise of preparing packups would take only a morning. We began at 9.00am but did not finish until 5.00pm. Geoff and I then needed to get ready for the bus run that evening. We enjoyed such laughter as the enormity of the task in hand tickled us. Each bag contained a drink, a scone, a teacake, four sandwiches, crisps and a piece of cake. We did 212 in all, one for lunch and one for tea!

On our journey to the seaside we stopped at the service station on the motorway, took out the huge urns for hot water, and gave each person a cup of tea. We would sit on the green in the glorious sunshine and enjoy our tea and cake. Praise God for we always enjoyed a day when the sun shone. In fourteen years of doing this outing we have always had fine weather.

When we arrived at Southsea we would give them all a time to return to the coach, hand out their lunch and leave them free to go where they wanted to go. Geoff and I would wander around the beach and the pier, to reassure them with our presence, buying them an ice cream, making sure that they all had suntan lotion on, as most of them had not thought to bring any with them.

One year, Margaret came as a volunteer, but was shocked when we went to buy the ice creams. As I went to talk to the ice cream vendor he asked me how many I would like. I told him that I needed 50 in the first batch. "How many? Did I hear right? You did say 50?" "Yes, you did."

Margaret's face was a picture of shock and horror. "How are we going to carry 50 ice creams?" I explained that we have a team. "Go and fetch some of the children over there. They love helping." It was a real challenge, nevertheless. Margaret's hands were milky white with melted ice cream by the time all 50 cones had been delivered safely. By the time the second batch had been bought, Margaret was a confident veteran of ice cream distribution!

In later years we made a decision to provide fish and chips instead of toiling over all those packed meals. We found an accommodating café right on the sea front in Southsea., who agreed to take all 106 people, prepare pre-ordered meals and serve us all together. Whilst some of our party sat inside the café to eat, the rest of us would enjoy our food in a covered patio area just outside – and all at a discounted price. Even with regard to our food, once more God had been before us and provided.

It was a joy to see the children squealing and splashing in the waves alongside their parents. It was another time for reinforcing the importance of families playing together and enjoying each other's company. In turn, it was obvious that the families had enjoyed and appreciated the day. Several of them would club together and contribute a small amount each to buy us a little souvenir from the seaside shops, with an accompanying card: "Thank you for a lovely day. This is the only holiday that me and my children will have this year." When I read this card it was heart-rending to realize these children would not enjoy the holidays we so often take for granted.

"Geoff . . . We've got some money left over. What do you reckon we should do with it?" A sharp intake of breath indicated Geoff's anticipation of what might be coming next.

"Oh, for goodness sake Steph. What are you thinking about now? Haven't we got enough to do?"

"Well I've been thinking." I noticed his "I'm-trying-not-to-listen-to-you" face. His pulling a deaf'n was becoming a habit. But I was undeterred. "You know, our people never get to go to firework displays." Geoff's hands go to his head. "And now it gets darker earlier . . . " Guess who came down to chat to us on the bus soon after that – a friend who owns a shop that sells fireworks, *and arranges and presents firework displays!* "We've got £350 left over this year. A friend of mine will let us have a field for an evening. I've had a look and it is safe because there's a fence to separate off the spectators from the fireworks. How many fireworks would I get for that, and how long would they last?"

"Not many, and it would last about 30 seconds!" My friend is renowned for his dry wit.

On the evening arranged we travelled in convoy in two mini-buses borrowed through Geoff's many contacts, and several cars provided by volunteers. The soup bus went too, loaded with soup, hot dogs, rolls and onions. Now I love fireworks. All those blazing, sparkles of colour setting the night sky aglow. It takes me back to my childhood. That evening I was really looking forward to the display. Guess what? I saw lots of fried onions, sausages and buttered rolls; I saw many hungry faces and heard the "oohs and aahs" BUT I did not see one firework! From my vantage point behind the cooker in the bus there was no view of the shooting, cascading pyrotechnics. Such is the lot of a servant of God!

"How can people treat their children like this?" Vanessa was tearful – devastated by what we had seen in the house we had just visited. We had taken clothing, food and bedding to a young woman and her four children. We had heard her demoralize her children over and over again, making them feel useless, inadequate, worthless. Those children believed what she was saying – that they were unloved and unlovable. Who was I to interfere? She was their mother. But the situation so touched our young volunteer that we were led to pray and talk about this family as we left the house. We could only do what we can to help. God has given us hands and hearts, and we leave the rest to God.

We meet people in the strangest places. The Holy Spirit leads us to people. We have no need to look for them. As we were putting furniture into one of the garages in which we stored donations, this young woman approached us and told us her story. She had been moved to Leamington from another part of the country. She was housed in a bedsit – one room for her and her four children to live, eat and sleep in. We were amazed to discover that her home was in the same building as the one we had rescued Ethel from a year previously. The old house had been converted into bedsits. What a small world! However, some of the tenants were still there from when Ethel was living there, for just above where the children slept was a picture hung over a hole in the plaster, and behind this aperture scurried a family of rats – lodgers with long-term leases.

Fortunately, the Housing Association moved her into a three bed-roomed house, and this is where we met her. Our storage garage was at the back of this house. We were invited into this filthy house and it soon became apparent that we needed to help. She needed provision of furniture, curtains, clothing, bedding and food. We found that the children were sleeping on floors. Of the most disturbing things we found were the children sitting like statues on a greasy settee, silent; too frightened to move or speak. We heard their mother degrading her children, trying to make us believe that they were the most evil children on this Earth.

This constant verbal abuse so lowered the self-esteem of these little ones that school was a toil. They did not attend regularly since their mother was often in bed when it was time to get them ready for the day. When they were there their minds were so full of the negative input given daily at home that they had great difficulty concentrating. This meant that they had low ability. They were low achievers. Absorbing their school lessons was a real problem for them.

After several months of visiting this family we took them to Wales on our caravan holiday. It was our aim to try and teach Mum that being a mother could be rewarding. I wanted to teach her how to be a loving mum who enjoyed the company of her children. Unfortunately, this holiday did not have the desired effect on this mother. We win some. Some we lose. We can only trust God. We have to let go of our disappointments.

As we prayed with Vanessa and Ellie our two student volunteers that night, I suggested that we might take the children out of their situation and give them a holiday for a week. They needed to be shown that they could be loved; that they did not have to bear a life of continual chastisement. Vanessa said that she had a house in Kent that we could use, and so we began to make our plans.

Mum was over the moon at the thought of not having her children for a week! Geoff went about arranging to use an eight-seater vehicle. I collected clothes for all four children, washing and ironing four sets, plus the bedding and the towels. Having two children of my own, preparing for a family of four was a mammoth task.

When the day came to go on our journey we picked up the children and were surprised to find that they had no luggage. Their mother had expected them to live and sleep in the one set of clothing all week.

We sang the choruses that we had taught them in Wales to help the journey go along easier. Then nine-year-old Tom chirped up: "Uncle Geoff! Is this the country?"
"Yes. This is the countryside."
A few miles on, Tom asked: "Are we still in the country?" Geoff explained that the countryside went on for a very long way. In amongst all the "Are we nearly there yets" we were asked: "Is the sea as big in Kent as it is at Southsea?" Such were the questions from

children who had very poor understanding of the seas surrounding our island. They had been kept in their home or went to school – that was the extent of their world. They were never taken to the park, or swimming, or the cinema, or even for a walk. They played just outside their home and no further. They were like prisoners in their own home.

When we arrived in Kent Vanessa was there to greet us. She was thrilled to see us all. As we started to unpack the car, eleven-year-old Molly took me to one side. She was very embarrassed to tell that she had started her monthly period before we had come away, and her mum had not provided her with sanitary wear, or any money to buy some with. At that we stopped our unpacking and went to the nearest shops to buy Molly what she needed. Whilst we were there we needed to buy waterproof shoes for the beach, buckets and spades, kites, games and toys. On our return we sorted out their sleeping arrangements, made up their beds, and sorted out their clothing into piles. Their faces beamed with delight at the thought that they had a clean set of clothes for each day, and clean socks, underwear and nightwear! They wanted to try everything on there and then! We started afresh, with a bath and a clean set of clothes, then sat down and had our dinner. For once these children ate a healthy meal – not the chips that they were used to.

Those children had a wonderful week. They delighted in the trips to the beach, in being allowed to run about, to scream and shout and play football, fly kites and paddle in the sea. At first they were subdued, not used to the freedom to be children. They carried fear on their backs like a mighty weight. But eventually, when they realized that there was no condemnation for behaving as a child, they began to relax and enjoy themselves. We took them to visit places of interest. I can still see their faces as they held the piglets at the rare breeds farm.

We have now lost touch with this family as they have moved out of the area. But as we sow seeds we can only trust God to water them; we can only pray that what we taught them will go with them into their adulthood. God called us to take these children away. It is hard to let them go, knowing what their home life is like.

"What good is it, my brother, if a man claims to have faith but has no deeds? Can such faith save him? Suppose a brother or sister is without clothes and daily food. If one of you says to him, 'Go, I wish you well, keep warm and well fed,' but does nothing about his physical needs, what good is it? In the same way, faith by itself, if it is not accompanied by actions, is dead." James 2 14-17.

Chapter 9

"But the Greatest of These is Love."

Believing in the importance of family life is one of the precepts that we try to instill into those we help. With those parents who have a negative experience of relationships, and the care essential to the smooth running of a household, it is necessary to teach and practice procedures, such as cleanliness, cooking, budgeting, schooling and childcare. When you have been taught these skills by example in a stable home life, it is difficult to imagine that there are those who do not know how to run a home. Time and time again we have discovered families that conduct their lives in such chaos that they have needed support in the most basic life skills. It has been our prayer on many occasions to break the cycle of unhealthy and unhelpful ways of life, for the sake of the children. We can only hope that in their own adult life they may remember some of the values and practices that they have been taught by us, and make decisions that are better informed.

And so we met and came alongside Susan – a young mother with eight children who had been subjected to a childhood of emotional depravation, sexual and physical abuse, and put into care.

Walking into Susan's house, and seeing her children running around with dirty, scanty clothing, my heart reached out. Here was a dysfunctional situation that needed input on several levels. And so our involvement became regular and consuming. We befriended Susan and her eight children, eventually supporting every aspect of their lives. Every day Susan and her children would come down to the bus to be fed. We provided clothing, shoes and bedding, curtains and furniture each time she moved house because existing furniture would be ruined. We took the whole family on holiday, and day trips I would take Susan and some of her children shopping, and for the occasional meal out, or for coffee – any activity that, hopefully would indicate an alternative to the degradations of the lifestyle she, and others, were used to. All this had to be done in a way that did not rob her of her dignity. She needed to know that we were there to offer help, advice and supplies, but we did not want to take over. In many ways it would have been an easier option to control this situation totally, but that would have been counter-productive. It was more important to show Susan how to deal with her own affairs, in the hope that she might learn to run her family more effectively.

Susan's children were our main concern, since they were the unwitting victims of their mother's background and habits. Not only were their physical needs plentiful, they also had experience of life that was irregular and disturbing in part. None of them slept in their own bedrooms, for instance, despite there being beds provided by us. They would sleep where they fell in the front room, either on the furniture, or on the floor, in the same room as their mother and her visitors. Hence those children were coming into close contact with drug taking and intimate physical contact between adults. They would witness noisy and sometimes violent arguments between their mother and her lovers. They never had a regular bedtime; they slept late into the next morning; their school attendance was poor. They lived in a house that was visited regularly by adults – the homeless amongst them - who knew that they could drink, smoke and inject in their home. There were stolen goods fenced in their home. The household was noisy and busy until 3 or 4.00am. Complaints from the neighbours were plentiful.

These children were experiencing the lifestyles practiced by their mother, just like Susan had done with her mother. How important it was to work alongside Susan and try to break the cycle, for Susan's sake, but also for the sake of her children.

Already, Susan had been advised that the children should start to have more regular bedtimes and should sleep in their own bedrooms. So the youngsters would be put to bed upstairs and be told not to come down. Consequently, when they needed to use the toilet, which was downstairs, they would defecate in the corner of their bedroom; they would cry and shout, having temper tantrums and kick the doors. Many of the doors in Susan's houses were kicked off their hinges and damaged, either by the children or by the many "visitors" to their home. Always there were dirty pots and pans piled in the sink; the walls had been scribbled on by the children; there would be a heap of stinking filthy washing in the corner of the kitchen floor. The whole house smelled and was in great need of cleaning.

Susan lost her home many times; each time we tried to encourage her to keep a clean and ordered household by renewing her furniture, fixtures and fittings, and each time she, her children, her men friends and her other visitors would damage and degrade the property. By the time Susan had been evicted for the fifth time, Geoff and I decided that enough was enough and I made my commitment to dedicate time and effort to helping Susan bring order into both her own and her children's lives. It would mean extending the help that was already given on a daily basis. The whole family still came to the bus for their tea each day, they still received bread each day and a bag full of tins each week. They all had clean clothes provided, and fresh bedding when needed. Yet they needed more. They needed daily contact with someone who would help them to run their lives in an orderly, clean, tidy, organised way; someone to help them to budget their finances; someone to show them that there were other ways to live than this. And that someone was Aunty Steph. I stepped into a known minefield, treading gingerly, taking with me the skills and knowledge that thousands of mothers and housewives learn from their own mothers and fathers. I stepped out in faith once again and fell – fell headlong in love with the most harem scarem family in a higgledy piggledy situation.

When Susan and her children had been re-housed for the umpteenth time into yet another property (she left behind one of several bed and breakfast accommodations), we decided that we would make every effort to give them all a fresh start. We worked hard to set up their home. After she had been in the house for only six months, six volunteers and myself removed and renewed the furniture, cleaned the house from top to bottom, washed and sorted all her washing, and removed all the rubbish. Geoff went to the tip five times with vans full of broken and useless items. The walls had to be washed down with sugar soap to remove the graffiti. Broken banisters and doors had to be repaired. I resolved to teach Susan how to do housework.

Once the orderliness of the home had been dealt with, I began to pray about what could be done to affect the lives of the children for their good in the long-term. It seemed that they had had their lives disrupted so much by constant changes of address and schools that to ensure a regularity in their day to day lives would be one way to help them in the long term. Therefore I decided to set aside a year when I would go each day, get the children up, wash, dress, breakfast them and take them to school. Thousands of people do that every day. What could be easier? Thousands of people do not have to contend with bad sleep patterns; with children who hate going to school; with children who are not used to having regular washes, or going to school every day, with a mother who would not get up much before midday. What a challenge! God help me!

Like a commander set to lead my motley troops into battle, I began arriving at Susan's house at 7.45am, in order to get them all up. Eventually, after much knocking at the door, someone would answer, and there they would all be, asleep in the one room with the light and the television on. I would then begin to make their breakfast of porridge, before dressing them. Of course, the fleas from the dog wanted to join in the fun. They jumped for joy into any passing breakfast bowl that happened to be placed on the floor, or onto any school uniform that ended up on the carpet. They were not happy to be taken outside and shaken off the children's clothes.

The next step was not easy:

"I am not going to school! You can't make me!"

"I will not get into that car!"

"I want to stay here!"

"Well, I'm sorry, but this is not up for discussion, so you might as well just get used to it!" This final retort from an exhausted Aunty Steph after I had worn myself out lifting three of Susan's children into the car, strapping them in and making sure the child locks were on the door. Susan's eldest child was more compliant. She was at secondary school, and was happy to be given the opportunity to live a regular school life. Her three younger brothers and sister did not share her enthusiasm!

"Aaagh! Take me home! I don't want to go to that rotten place!"
So the screaming continued as the teachers and myself battled to take
the children into school.

There were times when I would get up early, realising the battle
that lay ahead of me. On cold, dark mornings I would sometimes
want to stay in the warmth and comfort of my bed. The thought of
having to go and fight with Susan's uncooperative children made me
feel like giving up at times. Would anyone even be up to let me in
the house? How long would I be left standing, shivering outside their
house? How hard would I have to bang on the front door to awaken
them? My attempts at being inconspicuous were thwarted many
times as I was forced to pound the door, arousing the curiosity of the
neighbours, who twitched their curtains, wondering who was causing
such a rumpus so early in the morning. I was trying so hard to keep
Susan's dignity by being quiet, but it was not always possible.

I attended core group meetings, on behalf of the children,
supporting Susan in her role as a parent. I was ensuring their
attendance, obviously. Although they were very reluctant at first,
gradually the children became used to the early morning routine, and
there was then a measure of compliance over going to school. At that
time the children needed extra support within the classroom.There
were lots of issues regarding the behaviour of Susan's children
within class.

At home there were lots of areas in which support was needed.
Not only did Susan lack the skills to keep a clean and orderly house,
she also lacked the motivation. Although there is no doubt that she
loved her children, displaying that love in practical, helpful ways was
something that Susan had never learned. This, coupled with her drug
and alcohol use, meant that she was often not aware of the reality of
what surrounded her. Enter Auntie Steph, with a will to help improve
things for Susan, but, more pertinently, for her children. I tried
teaching Susan how to cook nutritious meals, how to clean and tidy
the house, how to keep on top of the washing. The task was hard
because I was trying to break bad habits in a tactful and helpful way.

By this time Susan regarded me as a mother to both her and her children. She had learned to trust me over the years, and knew that I had her best interests, and the interests of her children at heart.

But my involvement was not easy. Even journeys to school were eventful:

"Aunty Steph?"

"Yes darling?"

"You've got some fleas on your trousers!"

"Okay," pressing the button to lower the window next to Susan's eldest child, "would you like to remove them?"

Innocent citizens of Leamington Spa may have wondered what was being launched out of that car window as they stood waiting for their bus that morning.

Every day we battled against the fleas that had come from their unfortunate pet dog, and which were thriving in the carpet and furniture at Susan's house.

Gradually a sense of order was established. The daily school run became tolerable. There was some semblance of control surrounding that household. Unfortunately, Susan was perceived as being a very difficult neighbour; many complaints were levelled against her, and she was forced to agree to move once again. Although I admit Susan was not the ideal neighbour, especially because of her constant "callers", many of the allegations made against her were untrue. The neighbours would abuse the children verbally – they were even abusive towards Geoff and myself because of our association with Susan and her family. They would taunt and provoke her. And, being very verbal herself, Susan would retaliate with similar choice words. The situation was not helpful to anyone, but the neighbours were determined that they did not want "that sort" living near them, and rallied officialdom to rid them of this "nuisance". Lack of tolerance on both sides led to a young woman and eight children being put, once again, into bed and breakfast accommodation.

The council would not re-house her because, in agreeing to move from her previous home rather than wait for an eviction order, she had effectively made herself homeless.

After much searching of independent letting agencies and housing associations, I finally found a house that would accommodate Susan and her family. Deposits and a month's rent were required. We agreed to provide this money as long as Susan agreed to pay us back in installments. Other people heard about Susan's plight and felt it right to give some money to help her out. It was at this point in our relationship that I found it necessary to take control of Susan's finances. She gave me her benefit books to look after. When her money was drawn at the post office, she would pay me her monthly installment for the rental loan, and the rest of the money was then allocated to various bills and essentials. In this way I was able to help Susan to manage her money effectively. In the two years that I worked with Susan she was, for the first time, clear of debts. I persuaded her to buy stamps to pay for a television license. Similarly, she began to pay her water rates.

Once the family had moved into their latest home, I felt it was time to tackle the issue of personal cleanliness. Every day, for many weeks, it was necessary to wash, condition and comb through the children's hair to rid them of head lice. At first their backs were black with head lice as I combed their hair. I ensured that the children were bathed and that they wore clean clothes for school. The school and I worked alongside to apply to a charity to provide school uniform, and I took their uniforms home to wash and iron. Once their hair, their bodies and their clothes were clean and free from infestation, I would look with satisfaction at those children as they went to school. Susan's children began to take responsibility for their own cleanliness. Now they could hold up their heads and be proud of their appearance and their personal hygiene.

In this, as in many of our contacts with the needy, God's protective shield surrounded me. Not once was I bitten by fleas, or suffer the discomfort of being infested by head lice. We know that God had opened the door to help Susan's family, but I stand back in awe when I experience God's hand on my life.

The challenge of working alongside this family was absorbing of time and emotion. There was not likely to be a quick fix solution to undoing and correcting years of mismanagement and poor lifestyle. It was always going to be a long haul, but slowly there were tangible improvements being made. I believe that with continued support within the home in addition to that which I was providing, there would have been real and lasting progress.

Unfortunately, not everyone shared my vision. The progress was not fast enough for everyone involved and all the children were taken into care.

Just because I am a Christian it does not mean that I do not have to face stark realities, disappointments and the breaking down of relationships. I had invested heavily in Susan's situation – a vast emotional, practical and temporal investment for which the fruits are not obvious, but what I did was out of love, and that can never be wasted. I hold up in prayer each person from that family, from the mother who had very few of life's chances to the little boy who put his fruit salad into his coat pocket, and I leave them there in the care of He who knows why.

How I despair about Susan! How hard and long I have prayed for her and her family. I realised that I cannot give up on the people God gives us a burden for. I remember reading of the whipping boy – how in biblical times a prince might commit a misdemeanour, but his punishment would be given to the "Whipping Boy". His function was to take the punishment for his young master. Jesus was the whipping boy for us; the one who took the beating for our sins. It made me think how it must be breaking God's heart that He has given the most precious thing He has, and yet people are still sinning. What more can He do? There is still wickedness. There is still hatred. There is still neglect of others. There is still a lack of love one for another. I felt like the whipping boy for Susan. I had given so much of my time; of myself. What more should I have done? My heart was breaking. She was still on drugs. Her children had been taken into care. I felt like shaking her! She was not listening! I wanted to scream: "How much do you love your children? Please, please give up the drugs. Your children need you. You say you love them, and of course, I knew you did, so why, why don't you do something about it?"

Susan asked many times why I did what I was doing, and why I had not given up on her. She questioned me about my faith. I shared my testimony with her. She so wanted to be able to turn to God for help. She would seek, but not be able to let go of her past and of the habits that had controlled her life for so long. She attended an Alpha course, and made a dedication. All looked promising for a little while. As had happened so often, her old lifestyles had the upper hand.

I am often asked why I bother with people like Susan. They challenge me with questions such as: "Haven't you done enough? She'll never change."

But I feel I cannot put a time scale on caring for the ones we help. God has given me a love for these people that I cannot understand and cannot separate myself from. It is something that is a natural part of me – as natural as breathing is. On the outside, Susan and others we help live unattractive lives. They often present themselves unattractively. But we are called by God's love to see beyond all that. We are called to see what is inside – a lost soul in need of love.

"God sees what is on the inside . . ." Daniel

Chapter 10

Forget the Faces!

There was one family with which we spent a lot of time. There was a mother, Lynne, her partner and two of Lynne's children. Lynne was once provided with a bottle of bubble bath with which to bathe her two young children. She duly filled the bath with this foaming mixture, placed her two infants up to the neck in its deep warm suds, and left to soak, believing that no further action was necessary. It was hardly surprising that the little ones emerged spotless – up to the neck! Their faces, hair, ears and necks were just as grubby as when they went in the bath!

It may be hard for some to come to terms with a mother who does not know how to wash her children properly. But then we do not always know the full story when we judge. Knowing that story, I understand – but that is a story bound by the bonds of confidentiality,

Coming alongside Lynne on a regular basis meant that we grew very close to her. She regarded me as an adopted mother, and had vowed to follow me should we ever move out of the area. It was a joy, therefore, for us to see a great transformation in Lynne following a stay at a clinic for alcoholics in Wales. A former local minister had also worked alongside Lynne, and, together with us, we had discussed and arranged for Lynne to try this treatment. On return, the change in Lynne was evident. She looked pretty. The eyes that had once been clouded by an alcoholic blur were bright and alert. Her skin looked fresh; her hair clean and styled. For a while the hope was for Lynne to be a new Lynne, but the effects of the clinic did not last long; Lynne soon reverted to her old ways.

There was a sticky situation when Lynne broke her long-awaited dentures. Rather than wait for a dental appointment, she superglued the broken false tooth onto the plate, before replacing them into her mouth right away. Realising her predicament, Lynne did what lots of needy people do: she came down to the Mission bus - with her mouth stuck tight! She was not happy, but even unhappier when I told her that she would have to go to casualty to solve the problem.

When Lynne broke her leg, and was fitted with a plaster cast, she felt so uncomfortable that she locked herself in the bathroom in order to cut off the offending support with a carving knife. Having managed this vandalism, she soon realised that she was in even more discomfort and pain without it and so had to be taken back to the hospital to be treated for a second time.

Leamington Christian Mission used to provide a decorating service for the needy who had difficulty keeping their houses in good order. When Brian, one of the volunteers, came to decorate Lynne and Robin's kitchen, he pulled out the cooker, jumped down the back to paint behind it, but then discovered that he could not move. His shoes had stuck to the floor, welding themselves onto the layers of grease that had accumulated. Brian had to take off his shoes; leap back over the worktop; find his scraper; then return to the messy, stickiness and release his shoes by scraping the old fat from them.

Lynne's story is a confidential one – as are many told to us – but suffice it to say that she struggled with a horrific childhood, the memories of which chased away sleep. So she drank to help her sleep. Lynne's was just one of the families that we would, and still visit on a daily basis, taking food and clothing. We spend a lot of time listening to their problems.

Believing in the importance of family life is one of the precepts that we try to instil into those we help. With those parents who have a negative experience of relationships, and the care essential to the smooth running of a household, it is necessary to teach and practice procedures, such as cleanliness, cooking, budgeting, schooling and childcare. When you have been taught these skills by example in a stable home life, it is difficult to imagine that there are those who do not know how to run a home. Time and time again we have discovered families that conduct their lives in such chaos that they have needed support in the most basic life skills. It has been our prayer on many occasions to break the cycle of unhealthy and unhelpful ways of life, for the sake of the children. We can only hope that in their own adult life they may remember some of the values and practices that they have been taught by us, and make decisions that are better informed.

The Bible urges us not to judge others. Instead, we are commanded to love others as ourselves. When people do not have the same standards of personal hygiene, household cleanliness, or habits as us, it might be tempting to criticise; except that God gives us an insight into the hearts of these people. He allows us to see behind the dirt to the needs that must be met. If God loves the ones he brings before us, then, by His grace, we can be the servants through which that love might be shown. And thank God, He imparts a sense of humour; not to deride or mock the needy, but to see the funny side of the situations they find themselves in. It lightens the load. It lightens the heart. It induces a feeling of fun in what could, in other circumstances, be a tense, unbearable predicament.

Chapter 11

Pigs' Trotters and Imperial Mints

We read about God's miraculous provisions throughout the Bible. Manna came to sustain the Israelites in their hour of need in the desert. Nowadays, in Leamington Spa there have been heavenly provisions of the most appropriate and surprising things.

In the early days of the Mission we heard about a needy family who we went to visit. We took a food parcel for this mother, father and eight children. They owned their own house, but, on low wages and very high mortgage rates, they were struggling to make ends meet. The man of the house was considering walking out of the situation and his wife was becoming suicidal. Meat was a scarcity in their household. Even his favourite dish of pigs' trotters – that inexpensive delicacy – had eluded them. The children had no shoes for school. This family was at very low ebb. After talking to them we discovered a faith there, which under the circumstances, was faint.

When we arrived home, we had a message from a local pub offering food that we could collect at closing time that evening. The fare was both plentiful and sumptuous, provided in huge catering pots without lids. There were two saucepans of stew, some bread and two saucepans of . . . pigs' trotters! Needless to say, we drove back to that household, dicing with open topped pans sloshing dangerously near my white sweatshirt as Geoff drove enthusiastically over every pothole and bump in the town! The family were delighted, not just with the food, but also with the tangible sign that God cared for them. Who else would have known about that man's liking for pigs' trotters?

How great is our God! No one knew our telephone number in the early days. We were only ever known as "Geoff and Steph". Even our surname was not known widely. Our intention was for God's name to be glorified, not ours. So we do not know, to this day how the manager of the public house knew how to contact us. We did not know him. It's good that God did!

Working in the public domain – especially in an area where people give charitably – it often happens that we are asked how we cope financially. Leamington Christian Mission is not a registered charity; it is not funded by grants or lottery funds. It is funded by people giving of many valuable commodities – food, blankets, bric-a-brac, clothing, time, talents, money, and, most importantly, prayers. Similarly, our personal needs are met by a combination of our own private means and gifts offered specifically for Geoff and myself. With regard to both charity and personal needs being met, there are daily occurrences that happen too regularly and too particularly to be reckoned as coincidences. We have had surprising items of food included in regular supplies. There was the time when I mentioned glibly to Geoff that it would be lovely to have a haggis. That evening, just one was provided in amongst some sandwiches and cakes that we received. Never before or since has haggis been given.

I once saw a breadboard that I thought would be good for using on the bus. That evening, without me mentioning it, someone brought me the exact one.

I took a fancy to a plant, and that very one appeared.

Geoff likes mint imperials. So did my mum. She was very disappointed to discover that Geoff had run out of their favourite treats one day after Mum had had a meal with us. She worried that she might get indigestion after eating, and that a mint might help prevent it. So we sat, relaxing together in our lounge, which looks out into our back garden through patio doors. Imagine my surprise when I went out into the garden later and found a seven-pound jar of mint imperials sitting invitingly on our garden bench at the far side of the garden. We had seen no one enter the garden via the gate, even though it was visible clearly from where we sat. Such provision! We enjoyed mint imperials for months to come!

I had a fussy Persian cat. Before we started the Mission, and our income was healthy and regular, I spoilt it by feeding it fresh fish and meat. Once our new lifestyle came along, his diet was changed to "Whiskas" cat food. (Our money would not stretch to expensive fish and meat for feline gratification.) But it had to be a meat variety – the picky animal would starve rather than stoop to eating tinned fish based cat food. One day, as we were getting ready to visit one of the families in need, I found that we had no "Whiskas" left. I was rushing around running upstairs to fetch something before we went out. As I came down the stairs, I noticed a black bin liner in the porch. To my amazement, its contents were tins and tins of "Whiskas" – all meat! In those early days of the Mission, we did not share details of our private life. We were simply Steph and Geoff. No surname; no address; no telephone numbers; no information about pets!

We have had our hearts' desire met on many occasions. To me, it serves as a reminder that our God is a very personal God. He cares about us as individuals. What we want is important to Him. His provision shows that He minds us – that every little detail about us is noted. How humbling. How wonderful.

We didn't need these things. We had food; we had plants and breadboards. But these gifts touched us and blessed us. They were an encouragement; a sign that we were not alone in a work that is both a privilege to do, yet at the same time very demanding on every aspect of our lives.

There are other times when our needs have been met. There have been cheques made payable to Geoff and myself, offered for personal use, that cover the exact amount required for an electricity bill.

*****

At the beginning of Leamington Christian Mission we would travel to Birmingham City Mission once a week to share our food with them, and provide our volunteers with the opportunity to see how a larger mission worked. Returning one evening along a country road in our first bus, Geoff was in no doubt what to do. "Steph, start praying. We're out of fuel." The gauge read empty – not almost empty, but so far to the left as to be off the dial. Most uncharacteristically, Geoff had not checked the fuel supply before we had set off. We were miles from anywhere, let alone a petrol station! We could not contemplate pushing the huge, heavy vehicle. We had no spare can of petrol handy. Geoff was horrified to see that the trip meter told him that the last tank of petrol was finished. I did as requested. I closed my eyes and spoke to God, fervently. A few minutes went by. "Geoff, you had better let me hold the wheel, because you are not going to believe what is happening!" The dial was moving over to the right; it rested only when it read that the tank was three quarters full. That God-given supply of petrol lasted for well over a week after that. The trip meter showed that the bus had covered almost double its usual mileage.

*****

Geoff was in a hurry. He had assumed that he needed to leave home at 2.30pm, when in fact, his meeting in Coventry began at 2.30pm, and it was already 2.00pm. He jumped into the car and headed up the bypass in a rush. To his horror the car began to sputter and halt. Glancing in disbelief at the trip meter, just as he had all those years earlier, he witnessed the numbers reading a mileage on the limit of its consumption. The fuel dial was to the left of red! He had run out of fuel. He pulled over and prayed. He really had to attend this meeting with Warwick University students. He tried starting the car, grateful to hear the engine purr into life. Casting his thanks heavenward, he focused on the meeting, and what he was about to say. The meeting went well. He returned to the car, relieved that he had delivered his message on time, and set off on his homeward journey. So preoccupied was he with the success of the meeting that he failed to recognise, at first, how easily the car had started. Neither did he see immediately that the fuel gauge showed a tank half full of diesel. Again, the car ran for a further fortnight before needing to be filled up.

These experiences bowled us over. We stood back in awe at what God can do. How small I felt in God's palm. He cared for us. He cared that we should be safe and be able to carry out His work without obstacles on these occasions. The desire to share these miracles was great. But by telling of what had happened we came across incredulous people who asked why God did not put fuel in the buses all the time. Our answer is: we understand that God's provision is not for what we want, but for what we need.

*****

Again, there are times when God uses us in people's lives, and we are not always aware of the long-term implications of that contact. We have experienced "God-incidences" that we consider being miracles in themselves.

Many years ago a young girl visited the bus regularly. She was a drug addict. She was homeless. She felt unloved and unwanted. We fed her, clothed her, talked with her and prayed for her. Like many before and since, eventually she went her own way and we saw her no more. We sow seeds for God, but we so rarely see them coming to fruition. But God is so gracious. Recently we received a phone call from the pastor of a church that prays for us faithfully every week. His opening comment was: "Would you like me to bless you?" "Of course!" I answered. He started to say, "Our deacon says his daughter had phoned him to say that she had met this girl. She was on fire for God. She asked her if she would like to go for a drink, and her answer was 'No, I can't go for a drink. I'm a recovering alcoholic!' She started to share her testimony with her. She said that she had come from Leamington. She used to be an alcohol and drug abuser. She met these two people called Geoff and Steph, who really cared for her and they put her on the right road. She shared that she was going to the Christian Union. She was now doing her degree, and her life had completely turned around."

Of course, this was our erstwhile junky; of course, she just happened to be talking to someone whose fellowship at home had very close contact with the very two people who were there to serve her when she needed it. Here was another of God's gems. It was told to encourage us yet again; to tell us that we might not always see the fruits of our labour, but we have to trust that He will water and nourish them ready for the harvest.

It is not just phone calls that God uses. He also uses everyday situations. When my twin sister was receiving her nursing degree at Coventry Cathedral, we arrived and started walking up the steps. A young man called out: "Nice to see you, Steph and Geoff! You don't remember who I am." He introduced himself. For a few moments we did not know who he was. He looked so different. We remembered the young man who was at his lowest ebb, on drugs, homeless, downtrodden. This teenager had looked much older than his years. He was unkempt and unwashed, as if no one cared for him. But today he was there receiving a degree. He had overcome all odds. As he spoke we could see that the hand of the Lord had been at work in his life. I felt a sense of pride – like a mother's pride for her son – as I beheld this smart, clean-shaven young man, whose life had been turned around. Before us was a responsible adult who was making his way in life. Again, God had shown us the gathering of His harvest.

Just weeks ago we were praying in the bus after the evening food and soup service. We do this routinely for whomever we have encountered that night, for situations, for needs, to give thanks. We had begun to pray for one of our regulars who had reverted to drinking after many years of being dry. As we prayed, a deep feeling of panic and fear entered the heart of one of our volunteers. When she shared her experience Geoff rang the gentleman concerned, finding his answer phone switched on. Each of us in turn spoke words of Christian love and encouragement before the machine cut out. A week later it was wonderful to see the man down at the bus. He had not come to see us whilst he was drinking. He beckoned us to the side door of the bus. He had tears in his eyes: "I want to bless you for your phone call. I was at my lowest ebb when I received it. Your messages meant a turning point for me." God is marvelous. He works miracles for us, and through us. He knew what that man needed and allowed us to help him in a very dark hour.

The God of the Bible is the God of today. Bible stories were written so very long ago, and we read of all the miracles performed by Jesus. We may be tempted to think that they are not relevant – that they do not happen – nowadays. But we have been challenged by need, and God has been gracious. We have been privileged. We have received miracles. We have no other explanation. Time and time again God has met us in our need and has undertaken for us. I repeat: I stand back in awe at what God can do.

Chapter 12

The Older The Better

When our own mothers were elderly we would take them away on holiday. Seeing their need highlighted the needs of other, older folk we came across in the Mission. I began to realise that we take so much for granted – holidays in particular – that some people have never experienced. Ethel, for instance, had never had a holiday. When I asked her if she would like to go on holiday if we took her, we found out that she was frightened to go holiday. She was unlikely to be taken by anyone else because of the level of support she would have required. There were others like her. That brought us to our knees. As we prayed we made a mental list of the ones we thought would benefit from such a break. Initially we thought of sixteen older people.

Geoff and I decided to take these people away to the seaside for the week. Initially, we took a group of mixed aged adults, including some who were homeless.

But before all this could happen we had to find out how much it would all cost. Why do we worry? When God is in the situation we should know by now that all things are worked out to His glory – every penny was provided by His mighty hand. While I was searching for a hotel, Geoff was arranging transport. We hired a mini bus for our jaunt.

From searching out a hotel in Bournmouth to that initial venture, we discovered a warm welcome for our group of eighteen. We received compliments for being "such a lovely group of people". For almost a decade, Geoff, some volunteers and myself continued this annual week away. The owner of the hotel became so attached to us that he even offered Geoff and myself an extra day on our own – a welcome invitation to punctuate our hectic lives. He also grew to know more of Christ. What a bonus!

How many other old age pensioners like Ethel needed a holiday?

Eventually we began to take away the elderly – particularly those who had medical problems. So those with Alzheimer's disease, schizophrenia, alcoholic fits (from an old addiction), incontinence, cancer and heart problems, and some who had mobility difficulties all came on a trip to the seaside. The routine, once we were there, was a demanding one. Firstly, the beds would be stripped, and changed, if needed. I would go and wake them in the mornings and make sure they were bathed and dressed. Sometimes there was a reluctance to be bathed. Ethel ran the bath herself, and then sat in her soaking bedclothes telling me that she had already had her bath! Needless to say that excuse did not wash with me! Breakfast saw me sorting out and cutting up their food. Then we would go for a ride out and perhaps find a café where we could all have coffee, or a place where the more physically able could walk around the shops whilst the less agile could sit at the café table and watch the world go by. Or we may go down to the beach, for a paddle in the sea and a sit in the deckchair. Lunch was often at a pub where there were pleasant gardens; ice creams would be an afternoon treat. An afternoon nap was often necessary after that – for everyone concerned – followed by a cup of tea at five, a change of clothes then evening meal. In some cases our guests would enjoy the evening entertainment later on or a trip to the theatre; sometimes they would enjoy their meal and go to bed. All this was paid for through giving to the Mission. Once again He had given the vision, and followed up with the goods!

It was the little things that would thrill and excite our elderly guests. Ethel, for instance, was entranced by the crisp white tablecloths in the dining room of our hotel. She would gaze lovingly at them, and stoke their cool surface. God bless the person who heard us tell this story at a meeting and brought Ethel a crisp white tablecloth of her own.

The theatre trip caused great excitement. Some of our party had never been to the theatre before. Mesmerised faces mirrored oohs and aahs. Ethel was just like a little girl, watching the dancers twirl and leap in their beautiful gowns. The colours were breathtaking. Ethel had never seen anything like this before. Our guests joined in with the singing; they clapped with enthusiasm. The excitement for me was watching them having such fun. It was better then the show! It made me realise just how good God is. God cares about every aspect of our lives. I'm sure He loves to see His children enjoying themselves.

But Ethel did not want to leave the theatre. She escaped back onto the balcony seats, sitting expectantly after the show had finished, whilst we searched frantically for that sweet little old lady whom none of the theatre staff had the heart to ask to move.

When it came time to go back home to Leamington we had a rebellion on our hands, started by Miss Ethel, of course! She did not want to go home. "Can't we stay for just a couple more days?" Then everyone else joined in, pleading with us to stay for longer. We had commitments at home, so we could not stay. But, in her childlike way Ethel did not understand.

These holidays were very tiring; equally they were extremely rewarding, this was another way to show God's love. Not only children needed our care.

Chapter 13

Goodbye to a friend

Mary was an alcoholic. She was one of the ones we helped. She became a dear friend.

Mary had done so well giving up alcohol for months. On one of these occasions she opened up and told me a little about her life. Like most little girls she was brought up by her mother and father. But the difference was her mother had a drink problem and her father would end up looking after Mary and her mother and seeing to the needs of the household. Her mother's drink problem escalated, causing her father to say he had had enough of the situation and ask for a divorce. Her father had custody of Mary. She was five years old. Her mother had access to her on one day a week. As Mary grew she was able to go round to her mother's on her own. Her mother encouraged her to drink. By the age of eight Mary was in her first dry out unit. She had become an alcoholic.

Was it Mary's fault? People say to us "Why can't these people stop drinking? It's their own fault that they are in the situation that they are in today." But as you can see we do not always know the whole story. Her sad tale, unfortunately, does not end there.

Because of her alcoholism, she was taken into care. She lived with foster parents. Lots of foster parents are loving and caring. Mary found the ones who slipped through the net.

They made her climb through windows and open up houses for them to burgle. Her reward would be a bottle of sherry.

She grew and went on to marry. But the drink was still a problem. She had two children – a son and a daughter. She tried and tried to get off drink. She would go into dry out units to get herself sorted out. She would be good for a few months. Life's challenges would happen, the bottle would call and she would be back on the drink once more.

It was through the love of her children that she made a huge effort and came off alcohol. She tried to make a better life for them. She did not want history to repeat itself. Mary's home was lovely. She loved and cared for her children and all was well until her marriage broke up. Again the bottle became her solace – but not for long. She told me a few of the tricks that an alcoholic would play. For instance, when she returned from the dry out unit on one occasion, she told her husband that she was cured, and that the specialist had informed her that she could drink sherry without any ill effects. And her husband believed her! She explained that an alcoholic gets used to conning people into believing them so that they can have their own way. They are manipulative, determined to get their own way.

Then, one night, about 12.45am the telephone rang. A disgruntled Geoff answered it, upset at being woken from a deep sleep. When he heard Mary's voice, he assumed the slurred speech indicated that she had been drinking. I rescued the receiver and began talking to her to find out what the problem was. "I have phoned up to say goodbye. I have taken an overdose. I am going out. I don't want our Lucy to be the one to find me in the morning."

When I realized what was going on, I asked Geoff to phone the police on the other line while I kept her talking. When he had contacted the police, Geoff jumped into the car and went over to her flat. While travelling to her home I continued talking to her, discovering why she had felt she needed to call me. Some months previously we had sat and prayed and for reason known only to God He had brought it back to mind. By this time she was very close to death, and she had remembered the prayer, yet I could not.

We may not remember what we have prayed months before, but God can use situations to bring to mind the words that we said. This shows us that it is not of ourselves, but all of Him. Mary's intent was to destroy herself. God's plan was not fulfilled in her life yet; He was not willing to let her go. We never know when God's going to use a simple prayer.

As I spoke with Mary that terrible night I could hear the police and Geoff breaking into her flat over the phone. I hung up, jumped into the car and went over to the hospital. When I arrived the nurse was trying to persuade Mary to go into theatre to have her stomach pumped, but Mary would not hear of it. She was determined to die. Her son was to be married in a week's time and she could not bear the thought of encountering her future daughter-in-law's family. She felt that everyone would know of her alcoholism, and she felt ashamed. All she could see in her mind's eye was a tattoo on her forehead telling them all "I am an alcoholic". She was also frightened that she would be tempted to drink. It was all too much for her. The question that haunted her to the point of suicide was: "Will I let my children down?"

I just sat and talked with Mary, trying to reassure her. I asked if she would go into theatre if I went in with her. I told her that I would hold her hand. So, with permission from the medical team, I accompanied my friend into the theatre all the time praying very hard that I would not bring up my last meal before they had completed the grizzly task. Needles to say, it was not a good experience to be present for that procedure. It confirmed to me that I could never put myself in that situation. And yes, God *was* good – I *did* hold on to my dinner!

When her stomach had been pumped, the medics said that it was a miracle Mary had survived. With the amount of tablets she had taken, and the combination of drugs she should not have been alive. She had intended to do the job properly and finish her life, but God had other ideas. We arrived home at 6 o'clock in the morning, had two hours' rest then started our day, ready for a 9.00am appointment.

Mary did go to her son's wedding, looking radiant. She enjoyed that day, and many other days for years to come. She became a loving grandmother to three children. For eight years afterward lived an alcohol-free fulfilling life. Mary became a helper when we went on our seniors' holidays; she helped me lift a lady with cancer into the bath every day. She also helped on our days out to Southsea. She grew into a lovely friend and I could see the change in her inasmuch as she helped so many people. She would go shopping for an elderly neighbour, or do someone's hair when they could not afford hairdressers. She busied herself helping others and showing kindness.

The irony is that when she tried to kill herself, she failed. But, all those years later after she had shown kindness to someone, they rewarded her with a bottle of spirits. After being dry for years, the temptation to drink this bottle was too great. As she sat alone she drank sufficient of it to react with the drugs she had been prescribed for a medical condition, and the combination of the two killed her. It was a tragic accident, leaving us and her family bereft of a wonderful mum, grandma and friend.

Chapter 14

Friends and Family Matter

How much more, Lord? The work is so demanding. Mum's been so difficult today. This isn't my mum anymore. It's not only Mum – it's Geoff's mum as well; I've got to face her later. It's not fair. Everyone I love you've taken away. First Netta was diagnosed with Alzheimer's; now the two mums. Netta doesn't even know me now. At least I could have phoned her when I was upset. I know I can always turn to you, Lord, but human contact is so important to me, as you know. It seems so cruel, when she is just over fifty; her life seems to be ended in the natural sense. I need someone, please, Lord. Please heal them. Let me touch the hem of your garment and they can be made whole again. Then I can have my mum back again.

I could not stop the tears as they rolled down my cheeks and I sobbed uncontrollably, in the car as I came home from my mum's. Why oh why Lord is this happening? My mum has Alzheimer's, Geoff's mum has dementia; Netta, my best friend, has been taken from me too. I was sitting talking to God when I heard that still voice saying: "Steph, stop praying for the healing of your loved ones and start praising me for their lives." And as I started to praise God, I saw a picture of a book. As I turned the pages I saw my life before me; how my life would not be what it is today without my mother. I was reminded of how she framed my life, and how I would not even be here. Then I saw Geoff's mum entering my life and realized that without her I would not have Geoff. I also would not have had my daughter and son, and their husband and wife, and, of course, my wonderful grandchildren. As the pages of the book were turned I could see how God had led me to different people, including my close friend, Netta. God had a purpose for our friendship. Without Netta and that day that we talked about the vision, we wouldn't be doing this work today. How God used her! She taught me such wisdom over the years and I thank God for the time that we had together. Then I saw the words written in this book: "Let go and let

God." I remembered some years before; we were both in Netta's kitchen when she said those words to me. The words became suddenly real and went straight to my heart. In the same way God showed me everyone who had crossed my path – all those who had a part to play in my life, including those things that maybe we would like to forget. They make us the people we are today. It made me realize that as much as we feel that we want people to be healed, it is not always in God's plan for today. Praise God continually for the lives of our families and friends – and also our enemies.

We had been doing God's work in the Mission for seven years when we noticed that Geoff's mum was repeating herself and forgetting things. We would tell her something and within one minute she would have forgotten what had been said. Friends from her church were phoning to tell us of the silly things that she had done. They were concerned about her because these incidents were uncharacteristic of her nature. As time went on it was getting worse so the decision was made to talk to the doctor and have her assessed. We were told she had dementia of a mixed kind. Things became so bad that we were spending more and more time tending to her needs. This meant that I was going to her house at eight o'clock in the morning, and at least three other times during the day. We did this for about three years, until we became aware that she would have to go into residential care for her own safety. She would extinguish the pilot light on her gas boiler, and turn it off, and go around turning off every electrical appliance, including the fridge and freezer. Even though we taped over all the switches she would unpick the tape. Then she would turn everything back on and gas would hiss from her boiler. Of course, this could have caused an explosion if we hadn't been there.

It was so hard to have Geoff's mum placed in residential care. I felt like I had become her mother, and she the child. To make the decision to have her go into a nursing home; to dispose of her possessions – we felt like we were mourning her. We grow up with our parents making the decisions for us. All of a sudden the roles are turned around. You never expect to have to do this. We are not programmed to take the parental role over our parents. The person who was Geoff's mum was gone. This stranger had taken her place.

Within two years I noticed changes in my own mother. We all know, as we get older, we become forgetful, and repeat ourselves. But this was different. I could see history repeating itself. This was more than forgetfulness. Mum was changing, and we had to have her assessed also. As I spoke to God I remember saying how cruel this was. I could not cope with yet another loved one who was going to need so much care. "Lord, you know about my flag? Well I'm waving now!"

I have this imaginary flag that I wave. It has my name on it, and a message that says, 'Stephanie has needs too!' "I'm so tired, Lord."
My own mum had been diagnosed with Alzheimer's – and there was no cure; and I knew that things would get progressively worse. And they did. Mum died in May 2003.

During these years of caring for our mums the problems that accompany the work for the Mission still existed. This then was a very trying time. But God has brought us through. However, the stress of daily life took its toll on both Geoff and myself.

Geoff has struggled with back problems for the last ten years. Not only has this given him severe pain, it has also prevented him from doing some of the work he would like to do.

I was diagnosed with M.E. in January 2005. God has used this illness and showed me that if I will not slow down, He will make me! I thought I was Superwoman, that I could burn the candle at both ends and do the work of ten people! God had other thoughts, because He loves me far more than I love myself. He knows what is good for me. The first few weeks I was devastated, not understanding why God had allowed this to happen to me. Then I thought, "I'm no one special. Why do I think I am any different to anyone else?" I thought of all the people who were dying of cancer, whilst I was feeling sorry for myself. This realisation brought me to my knees in prayer. God can use this situation, and, yes God I'm listening. It was at that point that things started turning round. God led me to read books from our local Christian resource centre. It was through these books that I heard the voice of God speaking to me about situations that I had been praying about for some time, particularly about one family for whom I had a burden. So often I challenge myself, considering that people in authority know more than I do about dealing with some of the problem families. Through reading "The Kid" by Kevin Lewis, my eyes were opened, and I realized that my actions when dealing with this one family had been entirely appropriate, and that my knowledge and understanding of their situation had been fitting. Another book showed me that I had to walk in His strength, to consider that although I had M.E. it hadn't got me! Today I am able to pace myself and continue the work of the Mission.

We have entered into the midst of public domain in Leamington Spa. We are public servants whose boss has the highest authority. Yet the desire to meet the needs of others does not dwindle, despite the constant demands put upon us by the hundreds of folk we may be helping at any one time. Even though we sometimes feel tired, or ill, or stressed, the zeal we retain for their work returns after a period of refreshment. Even when we are on holiday we are in demand. Telephone calls about Ethel, or others whose needs demand continual attention, come through to us as we try to take a break away from home. We are stopped on the street when shopping in the town. We are woken during the night to answer emergency calls involving those we care for. Unlike many employees, we cannot walk away from our work place and find free time and space in the comfort of our own home. Our job is a 24-7 one; our employer is always on call, and He delegates His tasks to His servants. The difference between God and any other boss is that He provides His stewards with a powerful inner strength – the Holy Spirit. Without Him we would be disabled from our labours; we would have no energy, humour, patience, diplomacy, and faith to carry on. To us the task is simple: if there is a need, and we are in a position to help, then we will help, and feel humbled, yet gratified to be able to do so. It would not always have been so. At one time we would not have felt so inclined to drop everything and go where the need arose. But, once God had called, He gave us the ability and the desire to carry out His will. Our work is a response to a calling.

*****

Because our first responsibility is to God, we have found ourselves being contacted by a huge range of agencies. Hospitals and G.P.s, social services and social workers; the police; the Citizen's Advice Bureau; the council and environmental health, to mention a few, have all contacted Leamington Christian Mission to enlist our aid. I consider that it is because Geoff and I can act without having to be bound by the red tape that hampers other agencies. One Boxing Day, for instance, we received a call from a social worker who had been called out to a man who had such advanced scabies that his weeping sores had stuck him to his bed. She could find no other agency to come out and tend to his needs; to clean him and provide clean clothing and bedding. Yet this social worker knew that, wherever possible, we would do whatever we could to help. They had the highest Authority to answer to – not a man-established institution. We were available and willing to leave our Christmas break and go to the aid of that poor man, when others would have been bound by working hours and days. In another instance, hospitals have contacted us to ask for their help in providing food for someone who is to be released from hospital, but who, because they are on income support, and are paid once a fortnight, have no money to buy food. Again, environmental health asked for us to help an elderly man who was living in filthy conditions, where rats and mice were running across his lounge, and over him as he lay on his bed. Similarly, environmental health called us to a house where excreta ran down the walls and into the bath, because the plumbing was faulty. He too was plagued by creatures, including mice, rats and frogs. His bedstead held the plaster on the wall. A new bed was delivered to him, but within two weeks the mattress had become the nesting place of dozens of mice. Time and time again, this man had to have his mattress replaced.

"God, when you gave us this work you didn't tell us we'd have to get involved in all these different areas of work! Look at this diary, Lord! I've counted seventy-nine harvest festivals, ten Christmas carol services, several Women's Institute meetings, school

98

assemblies, ladies' meetings, men's meetings, Brownies, Guides, Cubs and Scouts. I've given up counting. You're going to give me a lot more strength than I got at the moment, because I'm not capable of all this. You know how long it takes to prepare for a meeting. I'm sorry, Lord. I'm moaning again. I know you always bless me through them. I love being used as an instrument. It spreads the word of the Mission."

There are times when we come across hostility towards the work. Not everyone appreciates this mission. There are a few people in authority that wish we were not here. They would like to think Royal Leamington Spa does not have a problem with homelessness and social deprivation. Such people challenge us, which is not always very pleasant. But God does not promise an easy road always. We are reminded once more of Paul's words:

"In all things God works for the good of those who love Him, who have been called according to His purpose."
Romans (8 v 28)

Then, out of the blue, we might receive a letter telling us that we have been nominated for an award, or been given the great honour of being invited to Buckingham Palace to the Queen's Garden Party.

When we receive the letters I feel so humbled that someone considers us worthy of the honours for which we have been proposed. What a lovely blessing God bestows on us through the generosity of people's hearts, as they support this work and seek to encourage us.

Recently, the mayor of our town honoured us with Citizens of the Year 2006, which we received at the town hall. This is not just recognition of the work Geoff and I do, in our opinion. We have a quiet army of volunteers without whom we would have far too much to do. We consider that the honour of this award is for all of the volunteers for all the work they do, which makes for the smooth running of the Mission.

We had a wonderful blessing at the gathering after the presentation. As we were talking to one of the councillors he said, "Congratulations on your award. The people of Leamington really appreciate you. I am a Christian, but my Christianity does not show how yours shows. You are really loved in this town."

At the time I found it difficult to take this compliment, but later, in the quietness, it gave me a warm glow of encouragement. I realized that maybe we do not always hear the positive feedback. Praise Him that He will send an encourager along from time to time.

God knows the time when we need a word of support, which in return gives us the strength to cope with people's problems. It gives us the resolve to continue when people are negative.

Chapter 15

It's Somebody's Birthday

"We've just got over the New Year, Geoff. I've got to start thinking about Christmas again. I'll take last year's book home and sort out what families we're going to wrap presents for. That room down the store is heaving with presents to wrap. I know it's only February, but if we don't start now, I won't get it done in time for the Carol service, and I'll be panicking!"

"How many presents do you think you'll be wrapping this year, Steph?"

"Well last year, if you remember, we gave out over five thousand! I think there'll be more this year. You know what these agencies are like. They'll be giving us more families to look after. I can't see these children without any presents."

"You are a big softy, Steph! When are we going to say enough's enough?"

"Ah, but Geoff, when you see the kiddies' faces when Santa gives them their presents it makes it all worthwhile. How can we not wrap up some more? Don't worry, love, I'll organize it. Me and my team will get cracking."

"God's so good to us. The churches and the school's came up trumps again this year. And the general public were generous yet again."

"I know I shouldn't moan. I know we need it all. Christmas will be much easier for these folk."

"Do you remember Jim. He was really depressed before Christmas, but said to Mark this Christmas had been his best yet since he'd been sleeping rough. He was thrilled to bits with that coat that we gave him. He couldn't believe that it was brand new. His own coat was letting in the rain. When he opened the other gifts, he felt like a little boy again. Mark had such a blessing from that man's pleasure. You can feel the excitement, coming from the ones we help."

"You're right about that. Mark told me that no matter how much time and effort he gives, the rewards outweigh giving. I agree. God's rewards never end."

"What date are we starting those hampers, Steph?"

"I booked it in the diary for Thursday the 6th of December."

"How many volunteers have you arranged to help this year?" asked Geoff.

"Dave's asked his gang of friends. I think there'll be around ten helpers all together with the Thursday gang. Mike and Jan will be double bagging. They'll be sick of putting one carrier bag inside the other by the time they have finished."

"Why? How many carrier bags have you given them to do?"

"Oh, about two thousand bags to start with! I hadn't better give them all of them or I might put them off!"

"Do you think they'll be strong enough for all those tins?"

"I know we struggled with sorting all the harvest festival gifts, but what a blessing they are going to be at Christmas. No one that we know of will go without food this Christmas because of the generosity of those that gave."

"It's a real affirmation that this is what God wants us to do."

"Ladies shouldn't have such muscles! No wonder after shifting six tons of food three times before it reaches the folk who need it!"

"What time have you arranged for all the volunteers to come down to the store for the great double bagging event, and all of the food to be bagged?"

"I thought 8.30am would be okay, don't you? You know Dave's a good time keeper, so it'll be best to get started nice and early, since there's such a lot to do."

"Come on, Steph! It's nearly eight o'clock. We've got to get down to the store if we're going to be ready for the volunteers at 8.30. Dave will be there waiting. And I need to get those tables set up. It was good of Paul to reinforce those table tennis tables so they'll take the weight. There's fourteen trays with a hundred tins in each – that's a lot of weight!"

"You know, we don't need to work these things out, Geoff. God provided those table tennis tables, and they're just the job, being extra large. That's all we need to know."

"Dave will have the same job as always. I've counted how many trays of beans etcetera so I've got my list. In the first bag, there'll be: 4 beans, 1 tomatoes, 1 spaghetti, 3 veg, 1 cooked meat, 1 sandwich meat, 3 fish, 3 fruit, 1 milk pudding, 1 tinned meat pie, 1 steamed pudding. So when the men have put all the first lot of trays on the tables, Dave will go round and put a number next to each tray, to say how many to put in each bag."

"I always think they should sing 'Ring a ring a roses' as they walk round and round those tables!"

"Oh no! Paula has other ideas! She'll want the Christmas Carol tape blaring away to get us into the Christmas spirit. You wait and see the faces on Dave and his friends. They'll try to get me to rescue them. I know exactly what Eric will say as soon as he sees me. He'll ask if I've got some mince pies and chocolate biscuits for their coffee breaks. Oh we do have a laugh! They're such a good crowd. I really enjoy the friendly banter down there."

"Have you sorted out what's going to go in the second bag, Steph?"

"Yes. Here's the list: A packet of stuffing, cranberry sauce, tomato sauce, chocolate biscuits, a tin of assorted biscuits, tea bags, a jar of coffee, a packet of pasta, jars of cooking sauces, jams, sugar, flour, cereal, a Christmas pudding, mince pies and a Christmas cake."

"You're never going to get all that in one bag, Steph."

"I know! We'll have to tie two together. God's primed the well again and look at all that's come gushing out! I haven't finished there, Geoff. There's another bag to do as well."

"What's got to go in there then?"

"You know – the stuff like washing-up liquid, washing powder, toilet rolls, toothpaste, soap, shampoo, kitchen rolls, Christmas crackers – and more Christmas crackers – squash, bottles of pop, cleaning fluids, bleach, furniture polish and cleaning cloths."

"Have you sorted out where it's all got to be stored, Steph, because there will be about fifteen hundred bags in all."

"When you've taken all the trays of tins from the middle room there will be space there. And the room where the freezers are will be clear."

"Oh, that reminds me, when will you have those freezers clear so that we can start collecting the turkeys and chickens?"

"Don't you fret, Geoffrey! It's all in hand. While you're organizing those hampers I'll sort the freezers out. I've got quite a lot of food in them ready for the Christmas party. When that's all gone there'll be at least four freezers ready for you. Carol's phoned me about the fruit and veg, too. That's got to be picked up a few days before Christmas. Everybody will have a Christmas dinner. And our poor old Ethel and her friends will be going to an organized dinner. I've arranged for them all to be picked up and taken home again. Aren't they wonderful? There's no time limit. Ethel can stay for her dinner, her tea and her supper if she wants and there's someone on hand to bring her home when she gets tired. I put my hands up to these people. God bless them for their kindness!"

"Isn't God good? He provides not just for them but for us too, that they won't be alone over Christmas, and we can have some time with our family."

"Whilst we're down at the store doing the hampers it will be a good opportunity with all of them there to ask for volunteers to load the hampers onto the buses, starting on the 10th December, and every day up until Christmas. Have you got your list for the helpers for the Christmas Carol service and party?"

"Yes, we're getting sorted. Anne's young people's group from the church will help with the decorations. They really enjoy making the hall look like Santa's grotto. They like all the banter and teasing that they have from all the other volunteers. They enjoy being part of the preparations. Have you organized a speaker? And remember, Geoff, we only need one this year! It was really embarrassing when we asked two last year."

Tony's agreed again to be Santa this year. Poor old Tony gets so hot in that Santa outfit, everything underneath it turns red! But he does make a good Santa. He's good-humoured and patient with the children. It was funny last year when you said to the children that Santa going and if anyone wants a hug to come up to the front. We didn't expect thirty children to come pushing forward to give him a hug. It really thrilled Tony to think that they had accepted him as someone they could approach and trust. It's fantastic to see the children's faces when Santa comes in. It's also wonderful when they feel they can give something back when they sing to us all. They request our special song, knowing that it's Jesus's birthday, and not just about receiving presents from Santa. It's good when this message has been heard and accepted."

*****

"Last year we had no presents at Christmas. Mum and Dad had no money spare after they had bought us our weekly food. Charlie at school boasted about his big turkey dinner, with roast potatoes and cauliflower and carrots and sprouts; with stuffing and gravy and cranberry sauce. I've never tasted cranberry sauce, and he can keep his sprouts, but I would have swapped him my Christmas dinner for his feast. I pretended that we had had the same, and hoped that he did not see the longing in my eyes as he and my friends went on and on about how much they all ate. They spoke of prawn cocktails before this great plate of meat and veg, and of Christmas pudding after it! I ask you! What I wouldn't have given for just a bit of that mouth-watering roast dinner. I was ashamed to admit that we had had beans on toast on Christmas Day, because my mum and dad could not afford turkeys and all the trimmings.

"This year, though, things are looking up. It started a few days ago when we went to Aunty Steph's and Uncle Geoff's church to a special service there. We had to get there early to make sure we got a good seat. So we had to wait a bit out in the cold and drizzle until some men in white sweatshirts opened the doors. They were all friendly and smiling and said "Hello!" and "Welcome" and "Would you like to take a seat?" We were glad to be out of the wet and start to warm up our hands and feet. The church looked lovely. It was light. There were flowers at the front, and pretty glass in the windows. The place was packed with people I'd seen down at the buses where we go for our tea sometimes. It was nice to see them all on their best behaviour. Watching all this took my mind off my rumbling tummy.

"Then Uncle Geoff stood up and welcomed everybody. They all sang songs about a place called Bethlehem and the baby Jesus being born in a stable. They sang about angels and shepherds and wise men. Then lots of us children were called to stand up at the front by Aunty Steph and we were asked to sing "Away in a Manger". Everyone else just listened quietly. I was a bit nervous because I don't know all the words off by heart and I can't read that well, so I couldn't tell what it said on the big white screen. Then Aunty Steph said that Christmas time was a time when we should think about Jesus's birthday, and have a good time; that today was like a birthday party to say "Happy Birthday" to Him. She also said that Jesus was given to us all like a Christmas present – the best Christmas present ever; and that we don't need lots of money to buy this wonderful present because it is given freely to us by our Father God. Well that's just as well because we don't have any money that doesn't go on buying food and clothes for our family. She said that God loves us so much that He sent His only son Jesus to save us from all the bad things we do. We sang this song that went:

"It's somebody's birthday
I won't forget,
As I open the things that I get
I'll remember the angels and the stable so bare
And Jesus who once was there."

"There's a lot to think about there, but it's nice to know that we have a God who loves us and wants to look after us. I'll talk to Aunty Steph about it next time she and Uncle Geoff come to our house.

"Aunty Steph and Uncle Geoff have been coming round to us for a few months now. It's a good job they did because we were all in a bad way before they started coming. We were all really, really hungry because Dad had lost his job and then he got really, really fed up and gave up looking for a job. Mum tried hard to look after us, but then she got poorly and couldn't do her cleaning job. So we didn't even have her money to fall back on. And we were all growing out of our clothes and shoes, and we couldn't afford the electric to run a washing machine or heat up the house, and, well, things got

106

really, really bad. Then Dad told us we were going to town one night to have our tea. I couldn't understand it. We had no money to eat out in Leamington. But it turned out we went to the buses next to those pretty gardens and we were given lovely sandwiches and tasty warm soup and tea. Then we had fruit and delicious cakes. Yummy! I hadn't had so much to eat in ages. That's where we met these two people who asked me and my brothers and sisters to call them Aunty Steph and Uncle Geoff. They had two special buses. One of them is set up just like a kitchen with work tops and hot water for making tea and for washing up. The other one is where we sat out of the cold. It had benches all round three sides so that people can sit down and be comfortable when they eat their tea. They are both painted white on the outside, with a navy blue cross and words that my dad told me said "Love in Action" and "Meeting the Need". When I asked my mum what those words meant, she said "They don't just talk about it."

"Uncle Geoff had a word with our dad to find out where we lived and he and Aunty Steph started coming to ours a couple of times a week after that. They brought us new school uniform so we didn't have to feel like tramps when we went to school. They gave us lots of food and clean sheets. They helped Mum and Dad sort out their money so that we could have some electricity again. All this cheered our mum and dad up. They started to feel better, and our dad got himself another job so he doesn't feel like a scrounger anymore.

"So this Christmas we came along to this church as a sort of thank you to Aunty Steph and Uncle Geoff. It made me think about why we had Christmas and why people make such a fuss about buying all those presents. I mean, why do they spend all that money on daft things when they could be buying food and clothes for people who are sad and poor and hungry – just like we were last year.

"Anyway, after the service in the church, we all went round to the hall at the back and I could not believe my eyes. All across two sides of the room were long tables overflowing with the scrummiest food you have ever seen. There were pieces of chicken and smoked salmon and sausage roll and pork pies and crisps and sandwiches and spicy onion bhajis and samosas and quiches. Then there were cream cakes and chocolate cakes and iced buns and birthday cake and fruit cake and chocolate biscuits and cups of tea and squash!

"After all that it was difficult to move! But we hadn't finished being treated yet! Oh no! We were asked to go back into the church and there was a lovely old man dressed up like Father Christmas who gave us all lots of presents. Some people ripped off the lovely coloured paper there and then, but not me. I wanted to save mine and have something to look forward to on Christmas morning – just like my friends at school.

"And then, as we were going home from the church, Uncle Geoff called our dad and gave him three big sacks of presents to put out for Christmas morning.

"Wait till I tell Charlie what I ate at this special birthday party! Oh, and this year I didn't have to pretend that we had had turkey and trimmings. We were able to tuck into our Christmas dinner just like all those other people – all those that don't have to open a tin of beans that is."

*****

There are those who have levelled criticism at those the Leamington Christian Mission has helped: "Why do they smoke and drink then come and ask for food? They could have used that money to buy their own food. Why don't they get up off their fat behinds and find themselves a job? They are nothing but scroungers! They don't deserve to be given all this stuff, and to take up the time of Leamington Christian Mission."

We realise that we could stand as judge upon those we see. The difference is made because of whom we see: a human being with need. They may need food; they may need a blanket. They may also need something more than material provision. From the number of folk that seek out the buses every day; from those who telephone us in the middle of the night, it is evident that they need a kind word; a smile; a word of advice; a prayer. Their needs go deeper than the things critics become upset about. Their lives are often broken and desperate. Some have reached the lowest point before they can bring themselves to come and accept hospitality from a soup bus. It is not as easy as onlookers would like to believe. One hour in the shoes of some of the needy might show them how it really is. The difference is found at the bus. Those working there are not judge and jury. They do not know the whys and wherefores of every person who finds themselves asking for food. They are told to serve, and this they do by the strength of God, and the love and example of Jesus as their guide. If they measured circumstances with the yardstick of the world then they too would stand in judgement of the visitors to the bus. Instead they have a higher, wider, deeper standard – one that is hard for the world to understand. The bus is a community within a community, where people can come and be accepted; where they can receive without question or rejection; where there are people who have been called to love and serve them.

Laughter is a regular and essential element on the bus, for instance. Being there is a joyful experience most of the time. If it were not, then, sandwiches and soup aside, people would not return night after night. For they catch the spirit of goodwill and keen humour. They enjoy the joyful atmosphere. Praise God for His smiles and blessings!

Chapter 16

The Last Chapter

I don't feel right. I'm so weak today. I really need a can. Look at my bloomin' hands! Keep still yer perishing nuisances! Stop shaking! I can hardly get myself out of bed to see to the dogs. They never used to get on my nerves. They've always been my pals; but for some reason I can't abide their snuffling and whining anymore. Poor things. They can't understand why I keep snapping at them. I can't understand it either, come to that. Mind you, I've got no patience with myself these days. I feel so tired. So tired. This place is filthy, but I can't be bothered to wash up or clear the dogs' mess away.

I've got to have a drink. Me tongue's sticking to the roof of me mouth. I suppose if I can't have a can, I shall have to have a cup of tea. I wish I could go down to the soup wagon. They'd give me a cup of tea and a sandwich. Someone would listen to me. I could have a laugh. That might make me feel a bit better; tell those ladies how if they weren't married I'd take them out. They don't mind a bit of teasing. They know I'm only joking, but I wish I could meet someone like one of those ladies who would look after me. I'd love to spoil them. How I miss going down there. All my friends – my only friends – we'd stand by the fence up against the Jephsons and have a good natter. And Geoff and Steph would always listen to my problems, even if I'd end up crying.

Ah well! Where are those perishing tea bags? I know I had some somewhere . . . Oh no! what's that? For goodness sake! Now look at my slippers. Flippin' dogs! Still, it's not their fault; I should have took 'em out. Now look, I shall have to scrape that off later. It can stay there for now. I just can't muster the energy at the moment. I'll have to sit down. Where's them bloomin' hankies. Me nose is drippin'; tears running down me face – and I call myself a man! What's my life come to that it makes me cry just 'cos I stood in some dog mess. Ok, pull yourself together and make a cup of tea. Milk?

There it is. Good grief! What's that smell? It'll have to be black tea again.

I need some grub. I've got to eat or else my sugar levels will be all over the place. I expect that's why I feel like I do now. Where are those tins that Geoff gave me at the bus on Friday? Good job I've got these else I'd starve to death. Here we are. Beans on toast. Thank goodness it's a ring pull because I can't find a tin opener. Bread? Yes! Green bread is just what I need. Just my luck. Just how my life is going at the moment. Everything I touch goes mouldy. My whole life is mouldy – rotten and stale.

Ooh I do feel cold. I'm frozen to the bone, and I can't stop shivering. I shall have to get back into bed under that duvet. Perhaps I'll feel better when I've had a rest. Our mother'd be horrified if she could smell this bedding. Oh how I used to hate how she'd change the sheets every week, and make me keep my bedroom tidy. But how I'd love to have some of her starchy white sheets. Whatever happened to me and my parents? How did it all go wrong? I couldn't wait to get out of that house – all that nagging to tidy this and put away that. Get your homework done and why have you only got that grade in your exams? What time do you call this for coming in at night. And is that cigarette smoke I can smell on your clothes? Have you been drinking? I'm sure I can smell beer on your breath!

Bloomin' hypocrites! When I think of all the parties they used to have in our house. All my dad's snooty friends from work. All their "My Simon is going up to Oxford next term. Where is Thomas going?" All the disappointment on their faces. They were always ashamed of me. Whatever I did was never good enough. Just because I wasn't as clever as some of their friends' kids. Bet they wished I'd never been born. I know my drinking was yet another disappointment, but it was the drink that made me feel better. A few cans helped me forget the look on their faces.

How was it my fault that they had their precious friends round when I came home one night? Okay, I'd had a few drinks, but if Simon hadn't been in the way when I was trying to get to the bathroom I wouldn't have been sick all over his new Armani creation! There was such a fuss made about that little accident. It was his fault in any case. Wasn't as if he couldn't afford a new one. He's got a wardrobe full of them. Still don't understand to this day why they had to kick me out 'cos of that incident. Our dad went overboard – saying I'd showed him up for the last time, and how I wasn't any son of his any longer, and never to darken his door again! Fine! I said. Don't worry about not having a son, because you're not my dad. You've never been a dad to me. Your job at the hospital has always meant more to you than me. You may be thought as a big man in your job, but they don't know how you treat our mum and me at home do they? Perhaps I should tell them one day. Let's see who's ashamed of who then!

So I left and ended up in this dump, but it was better than being on the streets. Thank God Geoff and Steph got me this. It's better than a park bench. Strange how things have come to this

I suppose I'm better off than my mate Dirty Joan. While I'm thinking of it – crikey there's a few that's gone lately. Blimey there's Fred, that Scots bloke, Doug, Nina, Lynne, then there's Double T. How many's that? Can't count up 'cos these perishing hands won't keep still. And I do feel sick. Oh I do miss Doug. He was a good laugh. We drank each other under the table many a time. In the end his liver packed in they said.

Then there's Lynne. Me and her didn't half used to fight, but I wouldn't have wished her death on anybody. She did suffer. In the end she'd lost that much weight that it was hard to tell it was her. The cancer was eating her away. And as yellow as a canary. They wouldn't let us in to see her when she went into hospital, but we'd sneak and have a fag with her when she struggled outside for a smoke. Managed to give her a can or two before we were spotted and she had to go back inside. Mind you, she wasn't on her own when she died. Might not have been mates with her, but there was someone there when she went.

What about Dirty Joan? Lived rough for years like the rest of us. Funny old world this. Smell her a mile away! How she ever kept a job as a PA to a high-ranking executive I'll never know. Mind you she'd probably have had a bath in those days before she developed an allergy to water! That's what she told Steve after he had run her a nice hot bath. Allergy to water my foot! Dirty mare! When I think how she'd just sit down on the pavement and tiddle herself. How anybody can abide keeping soiled clothes on like that I don't know. But then . . . look at me now. Look at this place. I've no room to call anyone else dirty. There were times when you could still hear Joan's la de da voice – sounded like she had a plum in her mouth. Not much call for a posh accent on the streets, though. Shame for her. No one should die on their own like she did.

And how could I have forgot poor old George? Only heard about him when I was last at the bus. Forgotten about him. He's been in that home for over ten years. Had that fit. Took his mind and had to be looked after like a baby. They said it was brought on by the drink, but I don't see how. Never affected me like that. A little drink never did anyone any harm. Mind you, his mum and family visited him, and were with him at the end.

I wish I had somebody here. It was all right when I was little. My mum would bring me some soup and a cold flannel when I was ill. She'd tuck me in and stroke my hair. She'd read me stories and give me cuddles. It was a lovely warm feeling. I wish she was here now. Why can't I be little again and snuggle up to my mum.

I am so cold. I can't feel my feet anymore. My hands are still now, but they've gone blue! What's going on? What's happening to me? Oh God! Are you there? How do I talk to you? I wish I'd have took notice of the ones down the buses. All of them people that help Geoff and Steph told us about You, God. But I didn't listen. They all find it so easy to talk to You. Why can't I? I know I've not done the things I should. I don't suppose You'll forgive me.

113

What was that Steph always used to say when I couldn't get to sleep and I couldn't stop crying? She'd say "Say the Lord's Prayer. You must have learned it at school. Say that, and it will help."

Our Father who art in Heaven,
Hallowed be thy name.
Thy kingdom come.
Thy will be done
On Earth as it is in Heaven.
Give us this day our daily bread,
And forgive us our trespasses;
As we forgive those who have trespassed against us.
And lead us not into temptation,
But deliver us from evil.
For thine is the kingdom,
The power and the glory.
For ever and ever.
Amen

AMEN

Epilogue

One of the services provided by us, of necessity, is the working alongside those who need help in managing their finances. There are those who have sufficient, but who struggle to budget their money sensibly. They need guidance to live within their means without running out. Therefore, we will offer advice so that it does not get spent all at once. We are trusted to look after the money of such ones; we are in a position to suggest ways of managing finances. And, if the money does run out, the bus will provide food so these people need not starve. How fortunate we are to be able to take control of our material possessions. Sometimes we may take this skill for granted; may expect others to have the same control; be scathing of those who do not. It may be more helpful to accept others for whom they are; try to help where possible; not judge when others cannot cope.

Helping the needy is effective when it is consistent and regularly present over many years. The intensity of support varies from person to person. There are those in Leamington who have benefited from the assistance of Leamington Christian Mission since it was first formed. Individuals and families have been fed, clothed, housed, received carpets, curtains, bedding, furniture, holidays, advice, comfort, prayer and friendship for fourteen years. On first meeting us, the contact may be daily, depending on their needs. But to ensure that the needy start to take responsibility and control of their lives, it has been essential to provide support on a supply and demand basis, whether that is late at night or in the early hours of the morning. Only when those contacted seem to be coping well do we ease off their assistance, on the understanding that they are always at the end of a telephone line. The commitment is tremendous because it is vision inspired. This is not a job – it is a way of life fired by faith.

Some of the needy have been served by Leamington Christian Mission since it was established in 1991. Others are relative newcomers to the bus. It is only through experience and prayer that we can gauge the right time to ease off, or cease the contact on a regular basis. Whereas some may need daily help with the provision of food, clothing and bedding, there is also the need for advice on financial matters for instance, or help with filling in a form, or guidance on how to approach the authorities about housing, or benefits, or college courses, or employment. The needs are as many as the number of people – each individual has a need unique to them.